Other publications:

The Key of Immediate Enlightenment (3 volumes)
Collections of lectures by Suma Ching Hai

The Key of Immediate Enlightenment:
Questions and Answers

The Key of Immediate Enlightenment
Special Edition: 7-day Retreat
A series of informal talks given during a retreat

Silent Tears
A book of poems written by Suma Ching Hai

I HAVE COME TO TAKE YOU HOME

A collection of quotes and spiritual teachings by
SUMA CHING HAI

Compiled by Sophie Lapaire
and Pamela Millar

ISMCHMA

Suma Ching Hai International Association maintains meditation centers throughout the world. These centers help people of all faiths and creeds discover the practice of an ancient meditation technique called the Quan Yin Method taught by Suma Ching Hai.

For more information, please write to:
ISMCHMA
P.O. Box 730066, San Jose, CA 95173   Tel. 408-292-9704

Cover design by Greg Parks
Original painting entitled "Filled with Grace"
by Suma Ching Hai

Printed in the United States of America.
First printing January, 1995
Second printing September, 1995
Third printing August, 1997

ISBN 1-886544-01-8

Library of Congress Catalog Card Number: 95-094064

CONTENTS

Preface

This book is a compilation of original quotes sampled from numerous lectures, interviews and informal talks given by Suma Ching Hai. Excerpts from oral teachings were gathered over the course of several years by one of the fellow disciples. What began as a sampling of her own favorite quotes given by the Master, soon became a voluminous collection of material. With the help of many fellow disciples who transcribed and translated dozens of lectures, a book began to take form. Through dedicated patience, devotional love, help from fellow disciples and the grace of the Master, this work is now presented to you.

The entire contents of this book are the original words of the Master, recorded verbatim. Editing has been done only on the order of quotes, and on the grammar and punctuation of the transcriptions themselves.

Through the spoken word, a living Master can bring ancient wisdom to life. To experience these discourses in person, the seeker is affected on all levels of understanding, beyond space and time, far beyond any mental concept. These type of Masters, having become fully conscious of their Supreme

Nature within, offer a perfect mirror of the most noble and divine qualities within each of us, a reflection of our own potential for self-mastery. As one comes into contact with this perfect image, one's life begins to turn away from fear and self-doubt and to move toward more tolerance and compassion, more hope and joy. Such is the experience that countless thousands have had in the presence of Suma Ching Hai. She speaks above and beyond general philosophy and theology, echoing the Truth which lies directly in the hearts of all seekers. This kind of experience is beyond the words alone, but rather an invisible connection all of us share with the infinite. Through her words, her eyes and her voice, one can obtain limitless blessing and inspiration. With her help and the practice of the Quan Yin method of meditation, one can quickly progress along the path to full enlightenment.

If the reader would like to further explore the inspiration provided by a particular quote, reference numbers are noted at the end of each quote which correspond to a bibliographical index at the end of the book. Within this index is a listing of the exact lecture dates and places where they were given. Corresponding audio and videocassettes of most lectures are available for sale through meditation centers worldwide. Watching and listening to these tapes brings one closer to the presence of the Master. In addition, seekers may occasionally have the great fortune of attending one of the Master's lectures in person. Periodically, the Master is invited to speak publicly in many parts of the world and these precious moments should not be missed. Entrance to these lectures is always free of charge.

Master Ching Hai is world-renowned for her great wisdom, sense of humor, humility and deep compassion. She has traveled to all parts of the world dedicating herself and her time in order to teach others that the Truth we all seek is not far away.

Her multi-cultural background (she is fluent in five languages) allows her to express one ageless Truth in a multitude of ways, so that each individual receives his or her own answer, according to his or her own needs. Through daily practice of a non-denominational meditation technique called the Quan Yin Method ("contemplation of the inner sound stream"), we can all attain understanding of the great joy, compassion and heavenly bliss described within religious and spiritual scriptures around the world. More than just a simple meditation technique, this living teaching brings to anyone who sincerely desires it the ability to carry the meditative state into all parts of their lives. It offers each of us a way to have true love and understanding for our fellow beings, to play our part in society while still keeping our mind clear of worry and attachment, and a way to find freedom here and beyond this world.

All of this, Suma Ching Hai offers free of charge and conditions to anyone seeking the Truth. She does not personally accept any donations, all of her public lectures are offered free of charge, and initiation into the Quan Yin method of meditation is given to anyone who is truly dedicated to their own spiritual development. Master says that a spiritual teacher should never charge the student for what they already own. She simply opens the door to our own inner wisdom and then guides and protects us until we have fully realized our own treasure inside.

May the Truth guide you along the path to your own Great Awakening.

Pamela Millar

Introduction

Every human being has, at one time or another, wondered about the deeper meaning of his or her life. We witness on a daily basis the suffering caused by our ignorance, often feeling helpless to change it. But we are also blessed with brief glimpses of deep insight and joy which bring temporary comfort and hope to our lost souls. Regardless of the tides and turns of our lives, the recurring questions still remain, "Where do I come from? What is the purpose of my life? What am I here for? and Where am I going after I die?" Should we search for answers to these questions, we would open the door to a multitude of philosophies and practices, some safer than others, some quicker than others, yet not an easy choice for anyone to make.

Searching alone may seem like wandering in a maze, not knowing what turn to take next. Countless road signs may seem to point in different directions, leaving us confused and constantly searching outside of ourselves. We seek relief from an undefined longing, a void which lays buried behind the distractions of our lives. But the day we find ourselves in the presence of a true spiritual Master, we know that the search has come to an end, for this living teacher proves to us that complete liberation and self-mastery is possible in this lifetime and we only need to claim it, for it is ours.

When we take away all that divides us from the world around us, we find that only love remains, and this is our true essence. Once a living Master introduces us to our own divinity, all of our previous illusions of self identity begin to fall away and instead of having to learn more, we begin to unlearn, to let go of useless, negative habits and ways of thinking. Our path is now set before us on our journey back home.

When a traveler is lost, he must find a higher vantage point in order to obtain a better view. The higher he goes, the wider and clearer his vision becomes. Soon, the ominous dark shadows that once petrified him are discovered to be only mere shrubs in the wilderness! Likewise, the higher we go on our inward journey, the more our fears and false limitations are revealed to us. We learn to see them for what they are and let go of them just as we would discard an old worn-out garment. As we shed the outer appearance of ourselves, we no longer see separation and we feel united with everyone. The color of our skin and the language we speak may vary, but our innermost fears and aspirations are identical. So as we get to know our true selves, we gain comfort and understanding both within and far beyond ourselves.

If you feel that you are ready to embark upon such a journey, this book should provide you with priceless guidance and blessings, much needed in our present times. Master Ching Hai addresses in a very specific way some of the most frequently asked questions posed by seekers around the world. She clarifies often misunderstood concepts without oversimplifying them. This collection of her teachings is very much like a practical guide to your own treasure hunt. It will provide you with an overall map, warning you of obstacles ahead, teaching you how to prepare yourself. With Master Ching Hai by your side, you will surely find your way home.

Bon voyage!

May peace be with you always.

Sophie Lapaire

1

Life on Earth

"Our life is like a dream that we haven't awakened from, and when our spirit is awakened we discover our real nature, no matter how long we have been asleep. During enlightenment we enter into higher levels of existence and we see life from a very different angle. Everything takes place very quickly, without effort or drama. Like in a movie, if someone dies, we know that it is only a movie.

We are all movie stars and the world is a great stage. We play roles life after life, sometimes as a husband, a wife, a minister or a queen and sometimes we play less desirable roles. And we play them unknowingly and ask ourselves why we have to play these roles, why such and such is on the throne and I am only a secretary. Those who are awakened know that the world is only a stage for us to learn, to fulfill our desires and needs, and to get closer to perfection." [16]

"The way most people live their life is not yet complete, and is not very ideal for gaining happiness and wisdom. There are many levels of existence and the first one is the physical level. Most people live their life on this plane, where the search for sensual pleasures is the main goal, be it love to eat, to sleep, to have all kinds of physical happiness, and we tend towards laziness too. We just work because we need to earn a living but we do not put our ideal and our heart into it. We usually do not like to work unless it concerns our welfare, and it is difficult for us to work for mankind as a whole.

The second level is what we call the emotional level. These people have very strong opinions and we can say that they are domineering or authoritarian. They are always right and expect others to do as they do. Many dictators or so-called great leaders of extremist movements belong to this level. Even those who have good intentions, when they make the wrong turn, they will not admit it and will not attempt to correct the situation. And there lies the danger, because of the lack of flexibility.

In the third level we live in the intellect, in the physical mind, which is, I am sorry to say, only a computer, an excellent one that can record everything and sort it without any intelligence and judgment. But without the intelligence of the soul, the mind is only an automatic machine. People on this level become generally closed in on themselves and bury themselves in any type of ideal. They are stuck in a way, not caring for what is happening in the world, without a real desire to improve it or to change themselves. They think that they are perfect the way they are, and many mistake this as being enlightened.

The next level is that of the soul, of self-realization, because we identify ourselves with the soul. We know that we and our soul, the source of inspiration and happiness, are one and the same and we know that we are not the body. We try to help the world and to help ourselves. But this is not the highest level, because we still have the ego and it knows its strength. Even when we say '*I and my Father are One,*' it makes two, and it is still too crowded! (laughter)

Then comes God's level, God's consciousness and realization. God is nothing but ourselves. While in the previous level, we thought that God was separate from us. It isn't easy to explain, but for the first time we act without thinking, without even knowing what we are doing. We become the author of everything without collecting karma. This is what Jesus was describing when He said '*I do not - my Father is doing.*'" [27]

Our Purpose on Earth

"Each one of us is given human life only for the purpose of realizing God. If we forsake this duty, we will never be happy in this life or in many other lives. To tell you the truth, this is the only reason for human suffering, and nothing else. If we realized how we struggled in our mother's womb, how we repented our past lives' mistakes, and how we promised God to utilize this present life in a very meaningful manner to serve Him, before we were born, then we would never waste one second to think of anything else but to try our best in all our leisure time to realize God!

But as soon as we are born into this world, we forget everything. Because it is the law of the material world to let people forget. Therefore, it is necessary that a Master come and remind us again, again and again, until we remember what we had promised to God, inside the womb of our mother. We might not remember with our physical brains, but our souls, the ability of our wisdom will remember."[31]

"Because God wants to bless the earth through us, we came down to be a link between heaven and earth. But because we have been exhausted and tired for so long, we have forgotten our great mission. This is why a Master comes once in a while to remind us of our true nature. This is why we are here."[50]

"Once we earnestly practice the exercises taught during initiation, we attain a balance between heaven and earth, being able to carry out earthly duties and to recognize the Heavenly Kingdom simultaneously. Since we have various earthly duties to fulfill, we should finish them as much as possible. However, our foremost duty on earth is to bless it so it may become a paradise, so that all living things can lead a pleasant life while developing simultaneously into higher consciousness step by step. In other words, we serve to aid in the evolution of the universe, awakening and using the Godly Power within us.

It is for this reason that we require the initiation that leads to immediate enlightenment, bestowing upon us the power that we can apply directly to best serve the world. Merely developing and unfolding bodily or physical power and offering it to the world does not suffice. That is why our world still remains as it is today, even though all of mankind is yearning for higher development and a better world. It is time we rediscover this, the greatest power in us, as soon as possible, so that our life on earth will change for the better, and the coming generations may grow up in a better environment. When we watch the present miserable state of our world, we discern only too well the absolute necessity for immediate enlightenment, not just to benefit us and our generation alone, but for the best legacy we could leave for posterity. That's true love in action."[52]

The Future is in Our Hands

"Everybody worries about the end of the world. Actually some people predict it and make many people worry. But even if the world comes to an end, the enlightened people would never feel bothered, because they know what this world is, and that it will go one day. But the life eternal always goes on, and nothing can affect it. Life eternal is what we are, wisdom is what we possess, love is what our nature is, and this cannot be destroyed, with any bomb at all. It cannot be limited by space and time. Therefore, the Masters initiate disciples without the limitation of space and time. Masters don't have to always be where the disciples are, but they can help them and bless them. The disciples will grow into mastership and also do the same." [45]

"In this age of many troubles and disasters we also have great hope, because God has ordained many saints to come into our world and their messages are almost identical. They say that we should seek the Kingdom of God first and then everything else will fall into place. Normally, we try to take care of worldly problems first, we take things into our hands, we try to run the universe, but we always feel very disappointed. The best political leader can only satisfy people temporarily and bring them some kind of material comfort. But we cannot take care of the whole world just with our political skills, or any other abilities. That is the problem. No matter how good our intentions may be, we have to first seek the Kingdom of God, the supreme power within us, and we are connected to it. That is why it is said, '*God made man in His own image.*' [1] Image doesn't mean our profile, body or way of life. It is the image of the invisible power that we are made of." [41]

"Even though we are enlightened, we cannot change the world. We can only reason and bring people into changing themselves. Therefore, we have to begin with ourselves. We cannot sit and wait for miracles. No one can change the world, not even thousands of Buddhas or millions of Jesus'. They would have done it if they could. Miracles do not happen in this way, where karma is concerned. We have to clean ourselves. We have to bathe ourselves. The best doctor can only give us medicine, but cannot take it for us." [26]

"We can save our world, instead of killing others for our own survival. We should rebuild our way of life, live a moral life, be a vegetarian, cultivate ourselves mentally and physically, and there will be immediate results. Our world will be changed at once! If everybody is planting trees instead of cutting them down, then we would be saved soon. Within ten years, the world would never be the same, without any problem. Truly there is hope, but only with the cooperation of everyone.

Therefore, I hope the people of the world will wake up quickly. I wish you would spread the message to everybody, telling them to save this earth together. Otherwise, what should we do? Heaven only accommodates the virtuous people. If the earth doesn't exist anymore, where will all the not-so-good people go? Therefore, we must spend some effort for the less desirable people. This planet earth is very precious. Should God wish to punish it, destroy it, there is nothing we can do but to comply with His will. However, if it still can be saved, then we should save it. It is because this world is a very good school, where many souls can come to learn and grow." [59]

"We are the co-workers of God. We have not yet achieved the wisdom of God, so we should respect His plan and His design because He is the 'Supreme Boss'. He knows what to retain, what to take away, what to repair, and what to destroy. Even if He destroys something, He makes it again; but when we destroy anything, we cannot make it again. That is the problem. It is because we are not wise enough and not powerful enough. Should we one day reach God-realization, then maybe we can talk about destroying and creating with our own hands." [20]

"God truly only gives comfort. If at this moment He gives us some sorrow, it is to remind us of the ephemeral nature of this world, and to remind us that we have to get back into the safety of the fortress, of the Kingdom of God. Anytime we forget God again, He will remind us. He will remind us in a gentle way first, and then if we do not listen to this gentle advice, He may push a little harder until He pushes very hard. So if you are now not pushed so hard by God, please don't wait until He pushes hard; and if He has already pushed you hard, please come back quickly to the Kingdom of God and enjoy all the comforts He offers inside." [7]

Q. Some people claim that they see great disasters coming to this world, and that millions of people will be killed. Is this real? What is your opinion?

M. It will be real if many of our worldly residents do not wake up and use their own saving power inside. God has given us a life-saving power but most of us don't use it. Of course, everything created will be destroyed in proper time. If we do not have enough creative power to restore it, then it will be destroyed. It is just like a house. It was built, but if we don't repair it, even when we have all the tools in the house, all the paint and equipment, but we don't use them, then the house will be pulled down or damaged by itself. Now in this case, even if it is pulled down or damaged, we have an emergency exit. If we don't know it and do not use it, then of course, we will be in danger. Therefore, I would like to offer you this opportunity to save yourself at least, should it come to that. But how many people will hear me? The thing is so simple, and unconditional. You just sit there and relax, just like when you sleep, and all the power will come to you, all the knowledge of your past memory will come to you, all the skills of life will come to you, and it is so simple.

But how many heed this? You keep asking me all the time about the end of the world. It will end anyhow if we die. So we might as well save our soul, and if we want to save the world, we have to contribute our power, the Supreme power. We have to take it back and use it, otherwise, who else can do it? The angels have their world, their duties to do. Jesus is teaching somewhere else, somewhere more advanced than our earth. Buddha has gone to the Buddha's land to do His things. Only we are here to rescue ourselves. If you are afraid of disasters, then get enlightenment, repair your house, restore your world to a more moral standard, a more enlightened planet. Then, no disaster will befall us. Otherwise, even if I don't know anything about the future, I could say yes, everything could happen. If the world is becoming so rotten a place, not fit to live in, then God will pull it down and create a new one. [41]

Q. How can an enlightened being who is living in a society which is in conflict help to remove that conflict?

M. It is very difficult. We can only remove the conflicts within ourselves. If everyone does this, there is no more conflict to remove. Therefore, even though Jesus was so great and Buddha was so grand, they could not remove the conflicts within their own borders, and sometimes the disasters affected their own lives. It is because the majority of the people in the world were not at peace, were not enlightened. Therefore, enlightenment is the only requirement for any illness of this world, for any war or conflict, nothing else is necessary. [46]

Q. Master, I am confused about what position to adopt when I see countries at war, being invaded, women and children being abused and tortured. Do you have any words of advice?

M. Your question is one of many concerned and considerate people, but there is no cure if people do not cure themselves. You know the law of karma. Suppose you succeed in killing the murderers and protecting the women. How can you do it in the whole world? And sometimes the innocent is not always so pure and the murderer is not the only one responsible. The whole society, the whole world is responsible. So what can we do? You can put that person in jail, but another person will come. We cannot change the world if people do not want to change, but we must try. Therefore, Masters go out risking their lives telling people to change themselves. So why don't you join them and light one more torch instead of sitting there and feeling sorry? Do something. Maybe you can save ten, maybe he can save twenty, and little by little we can save the whole world. There is no other way to change people, but to tell society how to change its pattern of life. Not to change the victim alone, but to change the whole society. And if we cannot stop the whole misery, we can at least stop some parts of it, and this is already a good accomplishment. [23]

Q. How do you see peace being established on this planet?

M. When everyone turns to their God-like nature again: do all good, think all good, and speak all good. Then it will be peaceful. Otherwise, there is no solution. No other being can give peace to you. We have to tune into peace, and live a peaceful life, and become an example of peace. When we become a living peace on earth, then there is no more need to talk about how to establish peace. [22]

Moving Beyond Earthly Love

"Our world has become sometimes intolerable. It is our own making. So now, in order to improve this or repair the world, or the house, the big house that we live in, with so many rooms which are the nations, then we should know that evil is avoidable. Evil is avoided by doing good, by keeping the commandments, by loving thy neighbors. But because our mind is so used to 'an eye for an eye, a tooth for a tooth', it is difficult to do what we think we ought to do, or to treat others in a very loving way. Therefore, we need a stronger force to help us, to pull us out of our habitual thinking and actions.

Everything in this world is actually also good for us, even evil. Evil is our mistakes. Fine. But, then we do not have to stay in the mistakes forever. At least the mistakes are a kind of shock. When we receive the effect of our mistakes, we will be shocked into realizing that this is not a proper thing to do. It causes us misery and unhappiness. Therefore, we turn around. And even all things in this world which are beautiful and enjoyable, are there to remind us of our true happiness within, in our true home.

Therefore, it is not a sin to enjoy the things that God created for us. But if we always feel very attached to these things, God will remind us that this is not proper. Therefore, we will sometimes experience unhappiness, or misery from the things that we cherish most.

It is wrong to deny the world. But it is not right to sink deep into the world all the time. Because we miss the better half of life which is spirit, which is more enjoyable than anything that this world could afford. Everything in this world is just a reminder of the true happiness, the true glory, and the true life that we should have and that we should know, because we have forgotten.

Many people ask me about woman and man relationships, and sexual pleasure, and all that. They ask whether it is sinful. I say: 'It is not.' But you should know that there are many more pleasures than that. Sexual pleasure is only a copy of the true pleasure when you are in union with yourself, when both forces within you, the feminine and the masculine aspects within yourself, are united. The union between man and woman is just a duplicate of that one.

So, God sends us into this world not without any instruments to remind us of the Kingdom of God. It is just that we have forgotten that these are reminders only. We just love the copy and forget the original. And that's what makes our life miserable. And even then, we could not enjoy the copy completely. Therefore, many of the man and woman relationships are rocky, and the sexual relationship between you is not that holy, not that mutually respecting, but it is sometimes abusing, and just a frustration release, a kind of instrument. Therefore, if we truly want to enjoy this life, we should enjoy the true life, which is a hundred thousand times better than the life that we know on earth. By knowing that life, we can also enjoy this life." [45]

"Many practitioners, maybe not knowing a Master, or not being initiated, or not having a proper understanding, or not yet having a proper practice, misunderstand that to be a practitioner we must put down everything and be cold to all relationships. It is not true, it isn't true. This is why in the Tao Te Ching, Lao-tzu says *Ordinary mind is the Tao*. When you achieve the Tao or enlightenment, the more you are enlightened, the more you are relaxed and the more you become very loving. You might not demand physical relationships with another person, but you just act in a normal way and do your duty. Anyhow, it is difficult to understand this, but you will in time. God is not so narrow-minded as to forbid us to love our husband or wife the way we used to. God is not so cruel as to separate a loving couple in order to attain Him. We must enlarge our heart to love God and also to include other beings, including our own family members. If we could love other beings that are distant to us and strangers to us, why can't we love our family members, our immediate beloved ones? Just be natural, loving more than ever before, then we keep our family harmony intact. Otherwise, if our partner is unhappy, it is difficult to be happy ourself.

In general, men and women when they are married, it is not only for physical contact alone, but it is for warmth and care, and in the name of meditation you must not abandon your partner with any excuse at all. Because that is your duty to show your love and care to another human being, and you have committed to that duty so you must do it. Loving another person is an honor, it is progress, it is not a degrading process. Understand? You have to love each other just like a Master loves you, even with or without physical contact." [35]

Q. Many Eastern religions have the tendency to view the flesh or the body almost as something to be discarded as garbage. I feel that when I came into this body, I signed a contract to care for it as best as I could, to make it function to live within the realm of this world. One has the powers of the mind, the God powers, but doesn't this require a sort of balanced view, trying to live well on both realms, as long as you live on both realms?

M. Yes, it should be so. It would be more balanced. What the religious texts mean is that we shouldn't overindulge in our fleshly sensations and desires, and forget the spirit. Sometimes it is said to an individual at that moment only, or to a group of individuals only, to people that need to hear that statement. Then it became a general guideline and it lost its meaning. When it was said at that moment, it was very strong and correct. But it is later recorded and given to other groups, and it is no longer correct. So, do what you feel like, but do not overindulge in any fleshly desires. How can you forget the flesh? You cannot starve the body and meditate. You must keep it, it means that you shouldn't always take care of the flesh and have no time for the spirit. Some people do that, therefore this statement is for them. Jesus also said to forsake the flesh for the spirit, but He ate and took care of His body as much as He needed. [30]

Q. How do I escape from my flesh, my love and desire for the opposite sex?

M. Don't get away from it, otherwise we will have no more children. Just stay cool and have one at a time. (laughter) Have one partner only, okay? If you have a soul mate that you find is good for you, and a three-dimensional love, physical, emotional and mental, it is fine. And then, the so-called fleshly desire will lose some of its strong hold on you after you regulate it with a stable relationship or within marriage. So don't worry, it is just the beginning. [46]

Q. Must one work or deal with sexual energy in order to gain enlightenment?

M. No, no, just relax. (laughter) All the energy and the struggle you spend to fight with your sexual urge, is better spent in meditation. Why should you torture your body so much? It is a natural phenomenon, and it will lessen its intensity with time. If you are married, everything, even passion will become very much lessened. The more you meditate, the more heavenly enjoyment you will find. Sex, I will tell you, is just a substitute for heavenly bliss. And because most of us lack the real pleasure, we cling to the lower substitute. But once we know the real thing, the other loses its charm. Just like when we grow up, all the toys, the plastic model cars have no more great meaning to us. It is because we have a Mercedes Benz, we have a Rolls Royce, a Cadillac, or any other car. We know it goes faster and is more useful. So don't worry about sexual problems, just get enlightenment.

After enlightenment don't fear that you will lose everything. You just enjoy things more intensively, but you know when and how, and do not abuse your power of enjoyment like you did before enlightenment. You might have sex now and again, if you wish and enjoy it. But enlightenment is your main aim in life, and it will never leave you after initiation. It keeps pushing you, you can't just not go forward, you can't just be ignorant again. And even if you have a little exercise now and again with your wife, so what? God doesn't care that much! (laughter) You fear too much of everything. Even a little sex scares you. Nothing is so scary! [46]

Q. What do you think of abortion, and when do you think that the soul enters the body?

M. Oh, you shouldn't have abortion. There is no question about when the soul enters the body, but it is a question about evil thinking, killing tendency. Understand? That is what we should abolish, the killing tendency. No need to ask me when the soul enters the body. When you want to have an abortion, you have killing tendencies already, and this is what we have to uproot. We have to cultivate compassion and wisdom and not lean toward the negative side of our nature. The more we lean there, the lower we become, the more we will be dragged down. You should also cultivate meditation and then one day you will also know when the soul enters the womb. There is no definite time, it enters when it enters. It may leave and come back again! So you never know when the soul is there or not. Even if the soul is not there yet, we already have this killing tendency, killing our own flesh and blood, and that is not good. If you kill an enemy or a fierce animal you have at least the excuse to protect yourself. But if you kill an innocent soul, don't ask... killing an innocent soul is not good. Please do not have such an idea, degrading yourself. Whatever difficult situation arises you can make it. Pray to God, find a solution, or give the child to an orphan organization. There are many couples in the world who want babies, they can adopt a baby. So do not have such an idea. [14]

Q. Is it possible to be fully divine and fully human at the same time?

M. Yes, a fully divine person is a fully human being. A fully human being is a fully divine person. Now we are only half human. We do things with hesitation, with ego, and do not believe that God arranged everything for our own enjoyment and experience. We separate sins and virtues. We make a big deal out of everything, and accordingly judge ourselves and other people, and accordingly suffer by our own limitation about what God should do.

Actually God is inside of us and we limit Him. We like to enjoy ourselves, but we don't know. We say to ourselves "I shouldn't do that." But why be vegetarian? Simply because the God inside us wants it. It is against our principle of not wanting to be killed. We ourselves do not want to be killed or have our property stolen. Now, if we do those things to other beings, it means that we go against ourselves, and this makes us suffer. You shouldn't beat yourself or starve yourself, for example. It is the same thing with killing. We shouldn't kill, because it is against the principle of life, and it makes us suffer, so we don't do it. It doesn't mean that we limit ourselves that way. It means that we expand our life to all kinds of lives, not just to human beings but also to animals. Our life won't be limited to this body but also extended to all the animals, and all kinds of beings. This will make us great and regain our grandeur. [30]

Divine Love

"Love erases everything, destroys all bad things, dissolves all boundaries. That is how Jesus cleansed the sin of His disciples, by love. When He was on the earth, He housed this love. When the Buddha was living, He housed this love for us to enjoy and so we could learn to love like He does, to learn to develop our love, to recognize and to eliminate all limitations in order to free our love again.

So they set an example. That is why people love Masters. They do not have anything else, they might not be good looking, or be young. It is nonsense to say that a Master should be a certain way. He could be a hunchback, but the love is still perfect inside that body. That is what attracts people. It is because we have this love within us. So when we see something similar in greater amount, we like to dive in and rub ourselves in it! If you are initiated in this kind of science, you will recognize your limitless love. If you practice hard and have faith, with God's will and grace you will have love like Jesus had, and become like Him. You can become a Jesus in a mini-skirt and high-heeled shoes!" [30]

"Jesus came and taught us that we must love our neighbors, and greater still, love our enemies. Buddha, Mohammed, Socrates, Lao-tzu, all taught the same thing. So I have come to this country also to remind you of the same ancient message:

How to develop this great love within you so that you can love your neighbors.

This love is invisible, but it is so great that we can feel it and we can use it at will. Why is the great force within called love? Because it forgives all our sins and cleanses all our sins. It does not matter what kind of wrong things we did before. If we make contact with this love, and know this love, we are clean like a baby. That is why it is called love. Love knows no sin, no boundary, no past, but only the present. Jesus used this love to cleanse the sins of His disciples. Buddha used this love to take people back to the Buddha's land. And Krishna of India, because of having this love, is still loved by the people of India and praised by them." [10]

Q. What can you speak about love, about the capacity that we have as humans to bring it down here?

M. True love, divine love? We cannot, except when we know God. Only when we love like God loves then it is truly love. Otherwise, it is only a portion of it. A portion of God's love comes between men and women, binds them together, makes them happy. A portion of God's love comes between a mother and child and makes them feel a very special bond. Similarly, a portion of this love comes between any beings, human or non-human being, and bonds them together and makes them happy. Could you imagine the whole portion that is being radiated in the whole world? That is why people feel comfortable in the presence of this kind of God's love flowing through a Master.

That is why since ancient times people worshiped these kind of Masters. That is why everyone followed Jesus, despite all the persecutions. That is why everyone adored Buddha. When people's levels were high enough to receive His entire love, they bathed in it, enjoyed it and didn't want to leave. So every time they saw Him, they couldn't keep their eyes off Him. It is because of this love that is within everyone but we just limit it by our own conception. Once we are free of all conceptions, love blossoms.

When we have no more ego, we become so loving like Jesus or Buddha and we attract thousands of people that never want to leave us. Meanwhile, they develop their own ability to recognize their own love, you understand? Before they only loved the one who blessed them with God's love. That is why they love their Master, only because of this love. The whole portion of love is housed inside the body of the Master. That is how all miracles are made, because the law of love surpasses all other laws, including the law of karma. Therefore the Master can free everyone that believes in Him, open all heavens, destroy all hells. [30]

2

Overcoming Obstacles

"Someone asked me recently, 'Why is God so powerful and yet He creates so many miseries?' God didn't create misery, it is our own human heads that have created all these. God does not make guns. God never made atom bombs. It is we who make these with our own hands. So if we stop that, there will be no more misery. It is we who do not share our property with our poor neighbors. It is we who are not diligent enough to spread the Truth, to spread the message of love, of charity, of endurance, of patience, of compassion, for others to listen." [13]

God only makes beauty. God made the flowers for us to look at. He made the sun to warm us, to shine on our world. He made the rain to fertilize our harvest. God never makes destructive things. It is only our own doing, our own negative atmosphere that brings all these disasters." [13]

"Once we understand why we suffer, we can change it. It is only when we do not understand that we continue. Similarly, when a doctor diagnoses a condition and knows where the sickness is, he can cure it; but the most important thing is that the patient himself should know how to live his life in order to stay healthy for a long time. In order to stay healthy in body, we should know some hygienic rules. We should know what food to eat and what exercises to do, so that we can prevent most diseases. In order to stay healthy in spirit, we should know what the Law of God, the Law of Nature is. We should know this so that we can stay healthy in wisdom and become 'God-like,' because God made man in His own image." [20]

"We have many prejudices, many so-called preconceived ideas about life, about enlightenment, about religion, about how we should lead our lives, about how religious people should be, about how an enlightened Master should lead His or Her life, about how He or She should dress, eat and even speak. I also had many preconceived ideas before, and after enlightenment as well. Before, of course more, but after a little bit of enlightenment it was less, and it will become less and less each day. God made me become more humble each day, until I had no more of my own ideas left, except God's idea. I have to do absolutely what He wants. Just like you, I had to learn by mistakes." [39]

"The more we know the less we understand. Because we accumulate too much mundane knowledge, we do not understand the true wisdom. So this is our crowded existence. We are too proud with our Ph.D. or whatever knowledge we gain in this mundane world and we forget that we are so much greater than that. Actually, when we are too proud, it means that we look down upon ourselves, because we are greater than that. Of course, knowledge of this world doesn't obstruct the spiritual wisdom, but if we cling to it then we are in trouble." [53]

Infinite blessing is passed through the eyes of the Master.

In appreciation for Master's aid in a time of need, African delegates present Master with a symbolic gift and a letter from their Master.

Following her lecture before the United Nations in Geneva,
Master enjoys the beauty of the Botanical Gardens.

Master is honored with an International Peace Commendation.

"As we grow higher into spiritual maturity, we become calmer and more placid in our thinking, in our life viewpoints. So people keep coming to us and asking questions. I have tried my best all the time to satisfy them. But still, it is difficult for some people to understand the answers, despite both our best intentions. It is because we are using our limited understanding faculty to try to grasp something which is beyond that. I also had many of the questions myself before, therefore I understand very well whomever comes to us and asks questions. It seems that they never have enough answers. That is how our mind is. We always feel inquisitive, because our mind is always inquisitive. It collects a lot of information daily, whether bad or good, because the mind doesn't have the power to discriminate. And most of our misery, dissatisfaction and prejudices, and many discriminations between ourselves and the subjects in life come from this inquisitive mind, which takes in all kinds of information and possesses it and makes it become its own.

So we should be careful of what we read and what we hear because if we do not select with discrimination, every other people's ideas and philosophy, sometimes which are not correct, will sink into our minds and become our own. And we will think it is us who thinks this way, who accepts this. And later, when some more information comes which is more correct and helpful to us, we will reject it or we will doubt it, because previously we had already recorded some theory which seems contradictory to the later one. So whatever we take in, we should first or at least later examine if these theories, teaching or ideals have any use to our daily lives or spiritual progress. Otherwise, we will have so much problem struggling between ideas, between groups and different thinking systems." [56]

"If we think that we are already good or excellent, we might be cheated by the mind. The mind loves glory, loves praise, loves fantasy, thinking that we are good. On the other side, the mind also degrades us. It might sink us into a depression and inferiority complex, and cheat us of our glory also." [34]

"Sometimes, we think that we are the doer in this world, and therefore we take all the burdens upon our shoulders. That is why we sometimes get exhausted, and then we get nothing done. If we get enlightenment, we know if we use it. If we know how to use the greatest power which is already provided within us, from which we came, and also to which we will return and in which we live our lives, then we will have less confusion, less and less each day, until no more confusion is left in our hearts, except to do the will of the Almighty. Jesus Christ also mentioned that *I do, yes, but not I, it is the Father in me who does it.* And in Hinduism it always mentions *not I but Thou.*

Before enlightenment, of course I had criticism in my mind. I also had dislikes and likes of how other people should live their lives. I had my opinions about many things in this world, even though they didn't concern me, and didn't harm me, and had absolutely nothing to do with me at all. I would even venture to criticize them or to try to make things right. And that is how we have been busy with our lives. After becoming so tired with criticizing the world and trying to make people right, I have come to realize that I am the only one who should improve, and everything else will be all right. God makes us learn by our mistakes, by lessons and by other people's examples. That is why I think the old Chinese proverb says that when we walk with two other people, or three people, one of them, at least one of them, will become our teacher, or is worthy to be our teacher. This is the truth that I have learned up to now. Because other people's mistakes also strike some memories within us. They remind us of something that we might have done in the past, and that we should never forget. We should learn from them to improve ourselves, and we should never criticize other people." [39]

"But I tell you, forgive yourself. Forgive yourself anytime. Whatever you do, just make an offering to God and let it be, whatever the outcome. Because we are not the body anyhow. We are not the action. We are not the doer of anything in this world. Even if we are, suppose we are the doer, we still have to forgive ourselves. We have to forgive ourselves when we make mistakes, or when we cannot help our habits like anger, or sometimes greed, or sometimes lustful thoughts. These things also arise from circumstances. It is not truly the Self, it is not truly the soul that desires all these things. So if we are angry with ourselves, we should be angry only with our habits, our accumulated habits. Or we should blame the situation also, not to blame the Supreme Wisdom, the real Self, because the real Self never errs, never makes any mistakes." [55]

Q. How can we liberate ourselves from suffering, from our painful emotions at the right time when we want so bad to let go of the lives, the circumstances around us? It is hard to see through because of the people we are attached to and we know that there is more to life itself than just ourselves and the love of someone else we couldn't let go of.

M. Just forgive yourself and try again. Sometimes, in some circumstances we are able to control ourselves, but with some great effort, and some other times we don't want to control ourselves, or we can't control ourselves. In either case, you just do what is good for you at that moment. Don't worry much about your emotions. They are only the waves on the surface of the ocean. It is not the ocean's fault. It is the wind, it is the rotation of the earth that makes the waves. So the ocean cannot blame itself all the time, and say that he makes the waves, that he makes trouble for the boats and for the people. He cannot help himself. [55]

Q.   How do you get rid of bad thinking?

M.   Yes, it is difficult. You must use your inborn power. You have to practice the Quan Yin Method, then you will naturally become pure. It isn't for us such a struggle anymore. Every day we use the light and the sound to purify us, to bathe us. But there is also a sort of inspection, a spiritual diary. Every day you check yourself to see how much cleaner you have become each day, in speech, body and mind. You see your progress. [5]

Q.   What is anger, why does it boil inside of us, and how do we release it?

M.   Sometimes it helps to release it outwardly. Sometimes between husband and wife, or parents and children there is some kind of tension, and after you have cleared it together, you clear the air. It is also helpful. Whatever comes naturally, just let it be. If you cannot control it, or cannot control it completely, just try not to bear hatred. Just express what you feel in the best manner you can. Because sometimes, anger when swallowed too much, will breed diseases within the body. So the best is that first we have the virtues of God and then all the passions, like anger, greed, or attachment will subside by and by. [29]

Q.   How would you explain or define fear?

M.   Fear is lack of faith in God. If you always sense God's presence everywhere and in all situations, then you have no fear. [22]

Q.   How do you deal with the fear of letting go of the self?

M.   I don't remember how I dealt with it. It just naturally goes away. By getting in touch and merging yourself with God, you just naturally have no more self. Slowly, slowly, the self will go out. That's it. I don't deal with it. To have to deal with it is a problematic thing because the self is very big. Therefore, let God deal with it. After practicing our method, you become less and less self, and then you become greater and greater. This is a paradox of God, because it is not for us to understand. [5]

Q. Dear Master, I always make the same mistakes that I don't want to make. I feel there are two of me inside, one good and one bad. How can I stop this?

M. Well, maybe this is the balanced proportion in your life that you need to learn. Actually, we can't be too good all the time. You will break! You see the man in the circus, when he walks on the rope? He has to walk this side, then that side. You know what I mean? One time he dips on this side, the other time he is siding to the other side. Otherwise, if he walks just like this, he will fall down. This life has two sides anyhow, one positive, and the other negative; one is happiness, and the other is misery. Sometimes, we can't help ourselves from dipping from one side to the other. It's okay! Forgive yourself. Try if you can. If not, forgive yourself.[55]

Q. Why do we have so much bad luck and difficulties? Is it arranged by God?

M. No, it is because we live in this world, and there is action and reaction. We create an individual cause and effect and also have a collective effect from the whole society and all the atmosphere. Bad energy creates accidents, catastrophes, disasters, illnesses, etc. Bad energy comes from our bad thoughts, bad actions and bad speech. Everything carries energy. Therefore, we have to be pure in speech, in action and in thinking. That is why we suggest the Five Precepts and the vegetarian diet, to purify our environment. [51]

Q. How do you explain rape, cancer and accidents?

M. Karma, cause and effect. *"As you sow so shall you reap."*[1] We do not see very far into the past. That is why we blame the present. There is nothing that happens without a cause, even though sometimes it is not entirely our fault. This world is very sad. That is why we have to find the way out. It is just like if you always drive your car on the highway, and if you do not find the way to the exit, sometimes your car may run out of gas, or you can have an accident because someone ran into you. [51]

Q. When people invade our psychic space, when should we surrender to it, and when should we fight it off?

M. Everyone has the right to his living room physically, as well as his psychic room. No one should invade other people's psychic space. Should it be done so, you ask sincerely that it should be gone. Ask the God power inside to help you. Protect yourself with the faith of your religion, but be faithful enough, be strong. Otherwise, we have initiation for you. Use the greatest power, and then everything will leave. In the presence of the king, no other topsy-turvy being can be present. [40]

Q. How can we protect children from being contaminated by modern life, television, drugs, laziness, arrogance, etc., and respect at the same time their so-called freedom of choice?

M. You can help them by selecting for them what is best on television and from their environment, so they can also have the freedom to watch television, but not the freedom to choose bad programs. Freedom is not always the best thing for children who have not yet enough intelligence to choose. When they grow up, you can give them more freedom. But above all, if you lead a life of virtue, goodness and beauty, you will be an example for your children to follow. [51]

Q. Why do drugs have such an influence over people in America?

1 Galatians 6:7

M. There are many reasons, some are visible, others are invisible. One obvious reason is that Americans have enough material comfort but still feel a deep solitude. In some areas, you can drive for miles and miles without seeing a soul, only freeways and forests. You might see a few scattered and hidden houses and almost feel like you are in a desert and very lonely. Communication with neighbors is almost non-existent so you feel lost. Time doesn't seem to go by and you do not know what to do with yourself. Your desire to understand the meaning of life, of death, consumes your soul and the pain is so unbearable that you take drugs that offer temporary relief and allow you to forget life's reality. People who drink or take drugs or any other toxic substances all do it for the same reason. So I never condemn those who take drugs. I only wish to help them and that is why I am here, to offer solutions.

If you feel that you are alone, if you don't have a real friend that loves you unconditionally, then you can always come to me. We will always be connected, and you will know that you will always have a friend. You might even see me appear, if you wish and are sincere enough. You will have won an eternal friendship, a guide with whom you can always share your joys and your problems, and that will always help you in the best of your interest. You don't need to use these cheap substitutes to comfort your soul. There are better ones in Heaven and they will be yours after the initiation. [24]

Q. Is it justified if I kill a murderer in order to stop his killing of other human beings. If not, what should I do?

M. Tell the police, because if you kill him, you are the killer and the police will be after you! Do tell the police so they can do their job. It is not your job, all right? But maybe this person will repent, so give him a chance. When he is in his jail, he might repent, or he might read some immediate enlightenment book (laughter) and then turn his life around. You never know what makes a person turn into a murderer. It can be many complicated situations. It could be a very intricate system of society, or some kind of trap he fell into and couldn't get out of. You see what I mean? So we can't just take justice into our hands without considering a lot of his background, and many of the previous life karmic nets between the different people's relationships. So sometimes we judge him unfairly. The murderer came maybe to kill those who killed before. And now, if you kill him, next time he will come back to kill you, and the devilish cycle never ends. So we had better not use violence for violence. 40

Q. So, there is no such thing as a completely hopeless being, no matter how many bad things one has done?

M. Every saint has a past and every sinner has a future. No one is hopeless. It is just that they don't know they were great, that they could be great again. And if they find someone who can show them their greatness, then everyone can do it. Even the one who killed 99 people and tried to kill Buddha to make a hundred, became Allajan. He became a Bodhisattva after the Buddha accepted him and initiated him into the order. 57

Beyond Evil

Q. Is there a solution to end aggressiveness and violence?

M. No, I don't have it. You have! Everyone has this ability. If we stop killing animals, if we stop all violent acts, the world will become a paradise. It is not only my responsibility, it is everyone's responsibility. Don't you think? Because if a

Master, any Master could do it, Jesus would have done it, Buddha would have done it a long time ago. [51]

Q. Is the idea of a dark force something in our mind?

M. Yes. We have free will, you see. We think in black and white, and Satan is born of the kingdom of God too, which is inside of ourselves. When we act against the good and true principles of life, we become the instrument of the dark forces. But the negative powers are okay too. They make life exciting and make life come into existence. Otherwise, we would all be sleeping in heaven! Nothing to do. But as soon as we are tired of the negative power and want to go home, we should. We cannot always play in the negative place, we must also go home. So my message is for those who are tired of playing, for those who want to rest and go home. That's all. Those who do not want to listen to me are those who still love the negative side of nature. [50]

Q. Does hell exist?

M. Yes, it exists, but mainly for people who are very disturbed in their minds. People who are virtuous and good never experience hell. For those who are initiated, never. Hell is a great hospital to help people whose spirits and minds are sick. It is similar to our hospitals on earth where illnesses are cured. [50]

Q. Are there such things as evil spirits, demon spirits or Satan that possess people?

M. Yes, there are such things. But many of the evil spirits are within the hearts of the people. When we generate hatred, when we generate depressing and oppressive thoughts towards other people, we breed these unpleasant electrical and invisible currents into the air, into the atmosphere. They condense together and become a force that is frightening to reckon with for whomever happens to pass by or comes into contact with that environment which is full of hatred, full of dark oppressive force. So it is better that we always think good, do good, and talk good, think God, do God and talk God, and to realize God is even better. [40]

Q. Satan seems to personalize evil, but is there an actual evil being or demon that roams this world, or is it within us?

M. The world within is also the world without. So we cannot really separate them. Whatever is in our minds will manifest outwardly. Therefore, two people in the same room will have two different perceptions of the same surroundings and of the atmosphere surrounding them. Do you understand? One may feel miserable to death, and the other one may feel joyful. So we cannot say that the evil is within or without us. It is both, just like God is within and without us and everywhere. It depends on our perceptions, on our conceptions. It can make God or evil appear. We must change our conceptions. If we think in a godly way and practice in the way of God, then we are always in God's presence. If we think and practice the ways of evil, then we are always in the presence of Satan. Satan is not a person with a personality. It is a force released out of our negative thinking, actions and speech. It exists everywhere. But we do not need to know him if we turn ourselves to the Kingdom of God. If we tune into the Kingdom of God then we are in it, and if we tune into the kingdom of evil then we will be in the kingdom of darkness. It all depends on our conceptions and our ability to tune in. So when we meditate, we use the technique to tune into the Kingdom of God, we are always in the Kingdom of God. It is just like a radio, you can tune into different stations. [30]

Karma

"All great religions talk about the law of karma. If not, why would they preach and ask us to be kind if our actions had no consequences? That is why the laws of karma and reincarnation are mentioned in all the great religions. Sometimes it is more clearly explained, other times it is implied. Our laws have been created to protect the order of society, and there are also universal laws to look after the order and the well-being of all the creatures of the universe. We do not only live in a country, we are also citizens of the universe and each nation is similar to a mansion. We must therefore know the universal laws and if we respect them, they will protect us from experiencing lower levels of existence." [48]

"Regarding the notion of karma, you must know that there are two types of karma: human karma and universal karma. Men's laws are governed by an invisible force that cannot be grasped by human understanding. This is called in Sanskrit '*karma*,' meaning the Law of Cause and Effect. It is mentioned in the Bible as '*What you sow, so shall you reap.*'[1]

There is good and bad karma, but both imply attachment for you on earth. After initiation, the karma from past lives will be erased, but the Master does not touch the karma from this life. If not, you would die immediately. We must stay here for a while to bless the world and to help our friends. Afterward, we can go to Heaven and return whenever, if this is our wish. Karma is an invisible force, very fair and strong. What we have created will come back to us. This is the law of cause and effect." [49]

"We have karma because we have this computer, the mind, the brain which is meant to record every experience of this physical world. That is why we have it. Bad or good we register it in here. That is what we call karma. What is karma? Just the experiences, bad or good, our reactions, our learning experi-

1 Galatians 6:7

ences in many lifetimes. And because we have a kind of so-called conscience, we know we should be good and sometimes we did bad. The bad things weigh down on us, just like a lot of garbage, or luggage. Because of the law of gravity, it pulls us down and makes it difficult for us to climb the mountain. Because of a lot of moral disciplines in this world, lots of rules, lots of habits of different nations bind us within these so-called conceptions of good and bad, guilt and innocence. Therefore, we interact with people of this world, and we have experiences of good and bad, guilt and innocence according to the customs, and habits of that nation, the laws of that nation. Understand? It becomes a habit that we think that way, that we do this, that we are guilty, we do that, we are a bad person, etc. And this is all recorded in here. That is what makes us transmigrate and makes us bound into this physical world or a slightly higher world. We are not free enough, light enough to float above. It is because of all these concepts and misconceptions." [38]

Q.   Master, you talked about what you call providence. Some of us could use the word fate for that, although providence seems to have a more spiritual ring to it. What about free will?

M.   That is the choice before our physical birth and during our physical birth. But after death, we can't choose unless we have merits which we accumulate during this life. For example, before we are born into this world, we have the choice to be a certain kind of person, but then when we come here, we shift that according to the situation and the persuasion of society. Then we lose the free will as well. We think that we are free, but we are not. [53]

Q.   So, the true free will, the true choice, the real choice comes before we even come in. Then we are behind veils or Maya, and we do not remember the agreement. Would you call it the contract?

M.   Right, the covenant with God, with our own conscience. [53]

Q. You spoke earlier about karma, do we have control over what we want to be in our next life, or will someone tell us what it will be?

M. No one will tell us what it will be, because it is our own actions and the fruits thereof that will determine what we will be in our next life. If you want to control your next incarnation, you must have the wisdom to find your own path and regain your own greatest strength. Then you will be able to have control. But now you are too weak. [24]

Q. Can we reduce our karma by praying?

M. Yes, we can, if we are sincere enough. Because a very sincere and deep prayer is a kind of meditation. We are in a meditative mood, therefore it reaches the deepest recesses of our grace, our merit and our storehouse of blessings, and it has an affect, it cleans. Only when we are truly sincere and deeply longing for forgiveness, then it helps. [24]

Q. Could we distribute our karma over several lives, so we suffer less each time?

M. Yes, you can do that, but you will suffer more. I will tell you why. Because each life we have karma already, and if you add the karma of this life, you'll suffer more only. Each life, you have enough karma even to spare, to suffer and if you add this life's karma, I think that you will suffer, more and not less. You understand? [24]

Q. Do the sins of the father follow the son?

M. To some degree, yes. We call this collective karma. It means the collective retribution within the family. On top of that, each one has his or her individual collective bad deeds or good results from good deeds. Karma means both good and bad actions and good and bad results, not only bad ones. Most people use it in a negative sense. [40]

Q. Dear Master, please explain what kind of karma it is for there to be dictators like Hitler, Lenin, Ho Chi Minh, who caused wars that killed millions of people, and made millions of others suffer?

M. That is the collective karma of mankind which, as I told you, are by-products of the inter-relationships between humans and other beings in this world or other worlds. And those kinds of by-products became a kind of very forceful strong energy hanging around our earth's atmosphere. And when it is too condensed, then it has to manifest into something visible, such as a very great dictator who kills millions, etc.

So therefore, these people are not to be blamed, in a sense. But, we ourselves are to blame. If each one of us had led a life of virtues, keeping the commandments, and refraining from killing of any kind, including the indirect killing of not keeping the vegetarian diet, then the world would never have bred these kinds of dictators in the first place. There are these terrible experiences to remind us of the virtuous way, and if we are not awakened yet, then these things will continue to remind us until the whole of mankind is awakened. [45]

Q. Could you address the issue of karma, how we dissolve our previous karmic debts, and how this relates to enlightenment?

M. Karma is a Sanskrit term for the law of *"As you sow so shall you reap,"* which is the law of the lower universe. When the Master gives you initiation, he pulls you up further. Therefore, the karma downstairs can be burned and does not affect you. He just leaves a little bit for you to carry on this life, which is already smoothed out and lubricated by the Master's power. After initiation, you have no more stored karma, so you don't have to be reborn again, if you don't want to. If you want to be reborn again, it is very easy. We can create karma or we can borrow it from many sentient beings to come down. Initiation is the destroying of all karma in the past, leaving no more opportunity for the beings to come back in the future. [46]

Reincarnation

"Reincarnation is a return cycle. If you have not found an exit leading you to paradise, you must go back. Just like on a freeway, if you cannot find the exit, you must return in order to find it. This is reincarnation." [51]

"The theory of reincarnation should not be taught, because we don't have an entity to reincarnate. What reincarnates perhaps are these clinging tendencies to the information we got, whether bad or good, and then that clinging tendency will go and find one instrument after another to satisfy our longing that we did not complete from our previous so-called birth. After the knowledge, the Wisdom or the God-Self that resides in this body leaves this temple, he or she will pass to another temple. It is like going from one church to another, we are still the same person. Actually, in the universe there is no one entity that exists. There is a mass of energy and a loving field, but sometimes it is divided into different sections. It is just like the electric current that is in the bulbs, in the wire, in the microphone in different shapes. It is in the refrigerator, a different shape again, and in the electric fan, but the inside current is the exact same thing." [56]

Q. What are your views on reincarnation?

M. There is no reincarnation. The soul never reincarnates. It is just our habitual thinking, our desires, our attachments that reincarnate. If we know the soul, if we are enlightened, if we know our connection with the whole universe, we are not reincarnated anywhere. We are never born and never die. But all this is theoretical talk. Just get enlightened and you will know everything. [41]

Q. If people are reborn, why is the world population increasing?

M. Because people are reborn! (laughter) Because most people are not enlightened and not liberated, therefore the world population increases. Because there are people in hells that come up to be reincarnated as human beings. There are animal kingdom beings, and after paying their retribution as animals, they come back and become human. The more beef, ducks, chickens and pigs we eat, the more overpopulated the world will be. Also there are some angels, some people from paradise who, after some period of many thousands or hundreds of years, will reincarnate again as human beings. Therefore, the world is always overpopulated. [6]

Q. Why do the Christian churches not accept the idea of reincarnation?

M. Because they misunderstand the Bible, and also because the Bible has been cut and censored many hundreds of times over. I'll tell you an example. When Jesus was asked, "Are you the reincarnation of such and such past saints?" He didn't say "no." Saint Paul also said *"I live, but no, not 'I' but Christ lives in me."* Okay? Now, if you don't believe in reincarnation, why are you waiting for the second coming of Christ? (laughter) Ask your church, then see how they answer you. [12]

Q. Is reincarnation a choice of the soul or spirit, or is it something that will occur without choice by the control and devotion of the Higher Power?

M. We have choice and we do not have choice. For average people, there is no choice. For Buddha, Saints, Christ, they have a choice. They consciously chose their parents, date of birth, place of birth and date of death, of leaving the world. They were conscious before they came to the world. They came by choice. They came to save the world, to help some of their friends, to help those who prayed to them for their help. But other people are compelled to reincarnate by their own deeds, their actions throughout past lives. Our thinking and habits form themselves into an energy, and this forces us to come into an environment to fulfill and to eradicate, if necessary. This already-formed concrete energy has to be diluted. [14]

Q. Is it the soul that carries karma from life to life?

M. It is the mind, the power of memory. It is a kind of energy force. When you do something, you create a form of energy that is invisible to your physical eyes. This energy creates a pattern that the soul experiences in this world, your ups and downs, etc. And after a long period of time, the soul identifies itself with this pattern instead of realizing that it is free from this pattern. [18]

Q. We are a product of evolution and thus I do not accept the possibility of coming back at a lower level, as an animal for instance. So that would be involution and not evolution, right?

M. Yes. It is evolution, but sometimes it stops for a while and then goes back up again. It is always going up but sometimes we slip down. If you want to go to the top of the mountain and your foot slips, you might fall down a little. But you will climb up because you know that you have to go to the top of the mountain, and how hard it is. It is always evolution. So if a man behaves as an animal and not as a human being then in his next life he will have to learn the animal's lesson because he has not done well. Then, he will be scared of it, will have enough of it, and say "Okay, no more. I will go back to a human life, I will behave as a human. I will know what to do next time!" [9]

Q.   I know of the law of cause and effect as a universal law. Could you tell me more about other universal laws? Are there more than one?

M.   Yes, there is a higher law than the law of cause and effect. It is the law of grace, the law of forgiveness which comes directly from God. The law of cause and effect is appointed by God to regulate the universe, but there are higher laws above this, such as the laws of love, forgiveness and grace. This is what Jesus brought down to us when He was in the physical body. And this is what any great Master would bring to people, whomever comes to them for refuge and help. This is the law of love and grace. [18]

Death and Dying

"Today I would like to talk about the most frightening but unavoidable thing: death. Among birth, aging, sickness, and death, the one we are the most frightened by is the last one, and it is unavoidable, isn't it? I will talk about what happens in dying for most people.

We have heard that our body consists of the five primary elements of metal, wood, water, fire, earth and soul. We are told that when we are dying, the soul will go out, depart from the physical body of the five elements. Further, the five physical elements will separate from each other, no longer combining together because when the soul is present, it acts like a magnet keeping the five elements together, just like the thread of a rosary joining all the beads together. If I remove this thread, the beads will fall to the ground. The same thing happens when we die. But we are not a rosary, because we have feelings. Why is death such a painful event? First of all because we are unwilling to leave this world, our relatives, friends, husbands, wives, children, fathers and mothers, etc. Secondly, because we are frightened of not knowing where we will go after leaving this world. Thirdly, because we haven't prepared ourselves, we do not know what to do when we die. Otherwise, dying is a very happy moment with nothing to be afraid of.

Many people teach us many things in this world: our parents teach us how to eat, and how to walk. Teachers teach us how to read and write and many more things. Doctors and midwives teach future mothers how to give birth, for example, how to take care of themselves, and how to look after the fetus so that birth-giving will be easier and not so painful. But no one teaches us what to do when we are dying. Nothing is mentioned. We can learn how to give birth, receive care when we become elderly with pensions and insurance. Doctors treat our sicknesses and teach us how to avoid or reduce the chance of being sick. But no one talks about death, and it is not good. Therefore, I will teach you tomorrow how to 'die.' (through initiation)" [2]

"All the functions of the body will stop the moment the soul leaves the physical vehicle! Just think, we spend most of our time focusing on this body and little or no time on the Real Self which is our eternal Beloved. That is why we need to distinguish the true man from his shadow." [52]

"The world is impermanent. Even if we learn a great deal, it won't help much. Great scientists also have to die, the most famous genius must leave this world and everyone will do it empty-handed. That is why all religious scriptures emphasize that we should not be so attached to this world. Why? Because if we only think about this world, we will have to come back to it, and if we think about God, we will go to Heaven. All religions teach us this, but it isn't easy to think about God.

You see, we prepare ourselves well for the birth of a child but why not for our death, which is the most important thing? When we have a baby, many people come to comfort us, but when we die, no one can be with us although it is the moment that we experience the deepest loneliness and suffering. Death becomes a painful experience because we aren't prepared.

Our body has nine 'doors', such as our eyes, ears, nose, etc. We can use any of these doors to exit the body, but when we die we will transmigrate again in the lower realms. Take a house for example. If you are leaving in a hurry through a window you may end up with many contusions. You must instead use the front door. But we cannot leave if it isn't open. There is only one door from which we can go to the higher realms. It cannot be seen with our physical eyes. Only the great Masters can open it. Since we cannot open it ourselves, we should ask someone who already opened his own door and will show us how to open it. Then we practice every day opening and closing it, and the day we depart we will have no trouble leaving.

I will teach you during initiation how to die, and afterward you will have to practice every day. If not, you will forget because you are too attached, too used to this world. All your thoughts go to your husband, wife, to your work and your boss. Take a nap and see how they immediately come to disturb you and make you worry. Therefore, we should save every day two and a half hours to practice 'dying.' During initiation, the Master will escort you and instantly take you to higher regions, and you won't have time to think about what you left behind. What you will see during your ascension will depend on the level you will have reached when you died." [2]

Q. Master, why don't we remember our previous lives and death?

M. Because it is too much for us to cope with, too much burden. We have enough to do today, with taxes, wars, children, and with our immediate problems and karma. Should you know that you have been such and such, very bad or very good, or very noble in a last life, it would be more confusing and you couldn't conquer the tasks at hand in this life. So God, the natural law, drew a curtain. You will know it when it is necessary. You will know it in time. And in meditation, sometimes you know it too, if it should be necessary for your progress. If it should not, then you won't know. Jesus also said, "*Do not worry about tomorrow. It is enough that we take care of today.*" [1] So if we don't want to know about tomorrow which will affect us, which is important to us, how much less should we know about the past which is already gone? You understand? [24]

Q. How do near-death experiences fit into your philosophy?

M. A near-death experience is truly also a death experience except that the so-called silver cord which connects our soul to our so-called physical instrument is not yet broken. So they truly have a death experience. Those who are virtuous and have a good conscience in life will see bright light and many beautiful dimensions, it is a true story. It is the same when you meditate, the only difference is that you can prolong this experience or have it again at will and extend it to a higher and higher dimension. So meditation is also an experience of death. Therefore Saint Paul said "*I die daily.*" You leave the body and go to a higher beauty, and you can come back at will with some practice, not very long. Some people get it right at initiation and continue ever after. [53]

Q. What lies beyond the cycle of karma and death?

1 Exact quote, Matthew 6:33

M. It is the greatest wisdom and the highest bliss that we can ever know. This is our real Kingdom, because beyond the law of "sow and reap," there is the Law of Love. Only love and bliss. And if we break through the cycle of karma then we go to that dimension where there is no life, no death, no karma, only happiness, only satisfaction. But by only talking to you like this, I feel that we are degrading it somewhat, because the human language is easily misleading and very limited. Even the ordinary love between a man and a woman, how can you describe that? [53]

Q. What happens to a person that commits suicide? What is the difference with those who die naturally?

M. Yes! There is a big difference. Most people who commit suicide are in a state of very low consciousness and great depression. The pressure of the world is too much for them. When we die in this kind of state of consciousness, we remain like this for a long time. This is not good for our soul. When you are so depressed, you want to get rid of the depression, but because of killing yourself, you stay depressed for a long time. [51]

Q. How should one treat a dead body, cremate it or bury it?

M. It depends on the landscape. The dead have already another abode, so the best is to cremate the body and scatter it into the sea where it belongs. [41]

Q. Why would a child have to die when he is so pure?

M. Because he doesn't need to live anymore. Maybe he went to Heaven. It is even purer. Sometimes, we have some work to do. For example, I have to stay here only three or four days, because this is the time I need to finish my work here. So I come for four days. And if I need to come again I will come again. Some souls have little to do with this physical world, so they come for a while, and then they go. They have sometimes a little karma to take from their parents, and then they have to leave. [51]

Q. If the purpose of living is to remember who we are, what is the purpose of dying?

M. The body was created to only last a certain period of time. Then when it is worn out we have to use another body more suitable for our learning.

Q. Is dying only for the body, or also for the soul?

M. No, the soul never dies. We just change clothes. After two days of wearing the same clothes, they get dirty, so we have to wash them. If they are too worn out, you throw them away and buy some new ones. So that is all. We just change our clothes.

Q. So we have consciousness and control even when we are at death?

M. Yes, but we cannot have controlling power unless we are enlightened and regain our greatness.

Q. Have you experienced death? Do you remember a death experience?

M. Well, I can every day! I die and I come back.

Q. Can I do that?

M. You can, and I will teach you how. I think that it was Saint Paul who said, *"I die daily."* When you are in Samadhi, you can sever the ties with this world for a few hours and then reconnect again. You come back because it isn't time to go. We must come back and finish our job again.

Q. Why do you want to die so many times?

M. I don't want to die. I just have to die in order to live. [24]

3

From Religion to Spiritual Understanding

"*I* do not belong to Buddhism or Catholicism, I belong to the Truth and I preach the Truth. You may call it Buddhism, Catholicism, Taoism or whatever you like, I welcome all of them. Many Masters have problems fighting preconceived ideas about all religions. I have none. I will tell you that all religions are good. All religious Masters are good, speaking the Truth and leading you to it. Stick to your religion and have faith in your own religious Master. If you happen to find a religious Master in this present time and in your own religion then you are lucky. If not, then search in other religions to see if there is any living Master available. But meanwhile have faith in your own religion, do not change to that Master's religion. Because all religions came from God and all religious leaders also came from God to convey their message in different times and places. All enlightened beings whether they are Catholic, Buddhist or from any other religion have all discovered the same thing, the same wisdom, the same ecstasy. I also found the same universe, and it is actually more a state of mind, of consciousness, of intelligence and higher understanding." [14]

"Buddhism is like Catholicism. I do not think that the teachings are different. When you compare the Christian's ten commandments to the Buddhist's commandments, it's the same: don't kill, don't steal, don't lie, don't drink alcohol or drugs, don't take another's wife or husband. And the rest of the teachings are only details and explanations, or historical events recorded by the disciples when their Master was still alive. In the Bible, for example, there are many accounts of wars, and tribes fighting each other. This doesn't belong to the teaching but because these events took place when that Master was alive, they wrote them down." [34]

"Jesus was a man, but Christ is a power. That power can be transmitted any time, any place, through anyone who is qualified. Just like electricity, it can go through any wire, if the wire is in good condition and there is a plug. You see, Jesus Christ is the Buddha, and Buddha means Christ. Christ is a Hebrew word for Buddha, and Buddha is a Sanskrit word for Christ. How about that! People never translated these terms in their own languages, they just used the original language and fought over it. There is always trouble because of the incompetence of the human language." [6]

"At the outset all scriptures encourage people to lead a pure life. *'Thou shalt not kill. Thou shalt love thy neighbor and thine enemy, not steal,'[1]* etc. The Christian commandments, the Muslim, the Sikh, the Hindu, and the Buddhist commandments are all the same. We shall be good people, loving to one another and purify the inner self. Now, the outer virtues we all know, and most of us can keep the commandments from the holy

1 Matthew 19:18

scriptures, but what about the inner purification and inner realizations which are mentioned? How can we hear God with our own being, without someone else telling us a second-hand story? These are more important questions than just our ethical conduct. Of course, an ethical life is a great help, and a must for one who strives to become one with God, to go back to the Tao, or to become Buddha. These all mean the same thing; to be united with the great source of all things." [7]

"Religion only points to the Truth, but we must find it with a living Master. Without a real Master, we don't even understand religion." [32]

Beyond Religion

"In Buddhism people believe that if they worship the Buddha, bow to His statue, light some incense, and offer some fruit and flowers, then they are safe and are taking refuge in the Buddha. I think that this is the most mistaken concept, because there is no doubt that the statues represent the past Buddha, but not the present. And the past Buddha cannot help us in any way except that He left behind some theory for us to follow and to examine. And some of us go to the church, get baptized, and get some cake, and we think that we are safe from the hell fires! Anyhow, I am glad that people do that because the symbolism of truth at least is well kept. Why am I glad? Because it shows how innocent people are, how easy to believe, how naïve. We are so innocent, so pure of heart.

So I am glad that the Buddhist people go to the temple and offer fruit to wooden statues, and I am glad that the Catholic believers go to church and repeat some of the ancient experiences thinking that they are safe. At least they show their purity and innocence. But innocence and purity cannot help us much if in this lifetime, we cannot see the Buddha or experience God ourselves. It is like someone just installed a telephone in your house without wire connections, and told you 'there is your phone, it looks like everyone else's telephone and that is it'. But what happens? You are just talking to yourself only. The connection is not there and the other end cannot receive anything. If we believe that in talking on one end of the phone, with no answer on the other side, that it is alright, if we get no response from Him, then it is even more innocent.

Before, I was that innocent. Every day I went to church or temple and believed that this was all there was to it. But then after some time, I grew up and felt empty, and I thought that God doesn't respond to anything and doesn't care if I pour my heart out. The Buddha doesn't dry my tears and answer my sincerest prayers and questions. He just sits there and smiles, every day like this. I cried, bowed and threw myself at His feet and He didn't move one inch! So then I became frustrated and then I became angry. (laughter) I thought how can you be so impolite! But it wasn't the Buddha that was so impolite, it was me who was so naïve.

So after some time, I realized that maybe the dead Buddha couldn't help me much, and I had to find a living one, a living Buddha inside me. Therefore, I started to look for Masters, methods and a real way to find enlightenment, not just bowing to a lifeless statue. So one day I found it after a lot of struggle, discipline, and effort. I have found what the Buddha had found. I have found what Jesus had found, what Lao-tzu, Confucius, Plato and Socrates had found. And these things I am willing to give to you free of any conditions or bondage. It is all free of charge, because what I discovered you already have. It is yours, not mine. It is not that I will give you anything. I will only help you to open it and show you where it is. Then you will find happiness and all sorrow will disappear. It is just like the Bible says:

'Seek ye first the kingdom of God and all other things shall be added unto you'[1]

All the scriptures emphasize that we find our own enlightenment, and all our sins will be washed away. It is as simple as the sun coming out and dispelling all the darkness.

Otherwise, we have what the Bible calls the sins from our own ancestors, or what in Buddhism is called endless karma from previous lives, and we can never wash it off by our own mind efforts. We could not do it by charity or good deeds alone, or by bowing to the statue of Jesus or Buddha. We must do it in the correct way, using the light of God, the inborn heaven to dispel hell's darkness. Jesus also said,Whatever I do today you will do even greater in the future. This means that He and we are equal. He didn't say, 'I alone can do all these miracles. You will never ever be able to do it!' No, He said, Whatever I can do you can do also. That is a great liberal attitude, and Buddha also said, I have become Buddha and you will also become Buddha. If we follow the correct method, just like with a scientific method, everyone does the same thing and gets the same result." [35]

The Forgotten Message of Christ

"Most human beings think that they cannot follow Christ's example, simply because they were told that they are too ignorant, too stupid, too helpless, that they are nothing. And because this brainwashing was perpetuated generation after generation, they ended up by believing it.

'He that believeth on me, the work that I do shall he do also.' [2]

Jesus didn't say that He was the only one that could accomplish all these miracles, to teach and to liberate people. He said that we can do the same and He even added:

'...and greater works than these shall he do.' [2]

So if Jesus said, *Whatever I can do today you can do also*, then why don't we start? We all want to become so great but we couldn't. Why? Because we are lacking power, knowledge and wisdom. It is just like a surgeon who has learned to operate on a complicated human inner system. If we learn with him for some time then we will become an expert like him. We can become as great as Christ if we learn what He has learned. That is very logical and scientific. There is nothing mysterious about becoming a Buddha or Christ-like. There is no need to go to the Himalayas, no need to shave your head, or wear different clothes. You can become enlightened in jeans! It is just a matter of different lifestyles.

But we forgot all about it. We believe what the Church, what the priests tell us, that we are sinful and without Jesus we will go to Hell! If Jesus were to come back again, He would cry His soul out because His teachings have been distorted and tortured in such a way. He does cry. He is still crying.

We forgot that the Bible says that we were made in the image of God, that we are His children and His heirs. It means that we are like our Father and that we also possess His power. If our father is a king, it makes us princes and princesses and that

2 John 14:12

is something, no? So why not believe in our value, why deny our inheritance, our birthright? We keep repeating, 'We are the children of God and were created in His image,' and we struggle every day to only earn a few pennies, and pray all the time without being answered. It is because we don't pray to the right source, and we knock on the wrong door." [17]

"The road to Heaven is difficult because,

'Narrow is the way that leads to life, and broad is the way that leads to destruction and so many will walk therein.' [1]

Some say that it is like a razor's edge, because it is so difficult to walk on. Why is the path so narrow? Because it goes against our way of thinking, our desires and our temptations. We must dive in the ocean of existence without getting our clothes wet. That's why it is so difficult. We must live in this world with all its temptations, its conflicts and remain disciplined and pure, like the lotus born in the mud, but so pure, immaculate and fragrant. We must follow its example and become a saint in hell." [5]

"When Jesus was alive He said,

'I am the Way, I am the Light of the world, as long as I am in the world.' [2]

So after He left, He is not the light of the world in a physical sense. So He has left us some teachings which guide us in our daily lives. This is very good. But there is something of a silent nature that we have not gotten. That is the silent teaching, that can only be transmitted through silence. And this is the most important thing that makes us see God and brings us nearer to God. So whomever can help us in this way, you should not feel guilty to come to Him." [56]

1 Matthew 7:13
2 John 9:5

Jesus and Meditation

"Now we see Jesus' life. He didn't go to church to pray, except when He went there to preach or to throw out the merchants or to scold the priests. I never read once that He prayed in a church, so what did He do? According to very reliable sources of research, we know that Jesus traveled to many countries, especially India and Tibet, and studied with many enlightened Masters from different schools. When you go to India truly seeking for a Master, you will find those with a meditative way of life, and they will teach you meditation. All of the Masters I know practice meditation, and the most famous Tibetan lamas do it too, in different ways.

So if Jesus stayed in India for at least a dozen years, then we can say that He would most likely have met some of these meditative Masters. He probably first encountered some of the less powerful Masters, who taught Him some mantras, some yogic exercises, how to do some miracles, like turning water into wine, etc. He probably learned these things in the earlier days, before meeting the so-called meditative Masters of the Himalayas. But even to do those tricks you must learn some kind of meditation technique, even though it might be only temporary.

When Jesus met these people, He must have then learned how to meditate. Otherwise how could He have shut Himself in the desert for forty days without a break? Could you just go suddenly in the desert for forty days alone? It is impossible except with training, with preparation before. For example, for those who practice our meditation technique, what we call the Quan Yin Method, meaning observing the inner sound, the 'Word' the Bible mentions that is the voice of God, we often do a seven days or a month retreat. For us it is very normal, but for ordinary people who do not practice our method, you won't be able to sit for five minutes, never mind five days. If you succeed in sitting for five minutes without moving your body and your mind, then you have already become a Master. So we know that Jesus went to the desert for forty days to meditate. We also could conclude that He has been practicing meditation techniques, that He has been doing meditation all along. And that was the last retreat He did before going out to teach the message of God.

Most Masters do that before they go out into the world, before they decide whether they want to take the cross or not. It is like the last minute when you hear the alarm clock in the morning, the last moment of enjoying the warmth of the bed. Similarly, most of the Masters, after having attained enlightenment, after they know that they have been assigned the mission of being a prophet of the age, or a Messiah, they will go into retreat for some time, just to prepare themselves physically, mentally, psychically to face the hard task ahead, and to walk the long road that God assigned to them." [30]

The Separation from God

"We are separated from God because we are too busy. If someone is talking to you, and the telephone keeps ringing, and you are busy cooking or chatting with other people, then no one can get in touch with you. The same thing happens with God. He is calling every day and we have no time for Him, and we keep hanging up on Him. This is how the separation takes place. Now, if you want to become reunited again with God, it takes time. Give Him one tenth of your day to communicate with Him and surely you will no longer feel this separation. But you know, we have never been separated. We all have God within ourselves. It is just that we are too busy, we blind ourselves with worldly obligations, so we do not know where God is. Just like when we have our glasses on and we look everywhere for them. If we are too busy we forget many things. I can unite you again with your God nature, so we need not ask why, but rather how to do so." [5]

"What makes us feel bound and 'un-free' is the tendency of clutching to this mass of knowledge or habits that we call 'I', and forgetting to look to the real thing."

The more we identify ourselves with material knowledge and possessions, the less we know how great we are. Some of the people who have a lot of intellectual knowledge find it harder to meditate, harder to attain the higher wisdom than the less educated persons. It is because they have more to wash, more to disentangle. Just like in a house, when there is too much stuff in it, it takes longer to clean out in order to bring in the new furniture. If you have only a few things, then it is quicker." [56]

"You may ask why, if we come from the Kingdom of God, would we have left it to be so miserable? We come indeed from an almighty universe, but we forgot it after the fall. Why? Because we have been wearing different clothes, and the more we descend the denser they become, and we can no longer see around us. If you decide for instance to go deep sea diving, you will have to wear a swimsuit, a mask, carry an oxygen tank, fins etc., and you will end up looking like a frog and won't be able to recognize yourself. As we descend to lower levels, we put on heavier and heavier clothing and instruments, so we forget all about the lightness we used to enjoy. The lower we go, the thicker it becomes and the more difficult it is to see things in a different light.

Similarly, when we came down we had to wear eyes, ears, mouth, fleshly clothes, all kind of things we didn't need when we were there. And if you wear it every day for sixty years you become used to it, you will identify yourself with these outer clothes. The deeper you go, the more instruments you need, and the more difficult it is to see the surroundings. There is no more sunlight just darkness, so we need artificial light. Similarly, when we dive into the sea of existence, we can no longer see God's light." [17]

The Return

"We have never been separated from the Most High, we have always been the Supreme, but because of our tendency to identify with the information we get, and the habits that we collect from the environment and circumstances, we have an individual, an identity which thinks itself separated from the whole. So after we are enlightened through our own efforts, or through a spiritual friend, we will see things differently. Then even though we still have an individual shell, we know that we are not that." [56]

"Now, if we want to see this light again, we must go up ourselves, or someone else will have to bring us up if we run out of oxygen, or if we are caught in some rock. So we must go through all the obstacles. Whatever you came down through, you must go up through. We will then be able to take off our equipment and regain our original beauty. We thus came from a superior world and dove in the ocean of existence to explore and entertain ourselves. The new world filled us with excitement and we forgot that the clock is running and that our life is in danger because when our mission is over we must return to the beach. And if we do not get out, a friend must dive in to take us back. Similarly, we have stayed too long in our equipment and have identified with our physical form. Now, to go back home to the Kingdom of God, we must go through all the levels of consciousness in the ocean of existence, however difficult it is.

Going down is relatively effortless because we are fresh, ready to embark on any adventure. Everything is new, so we descend very quickly without feeling tired at all. But when we have to go back up, it is another story! We are exhausted, running almost out of oxygen, and we have forgotten our way up because we were a little too adventurous. But luckily, our Creator has provided us with a connecting line. Have you ever heard of the silver chord? That is our saving line and when we strike it, it makes some kind of music that will guide us back home safely.

Our good friends Jesus and Buddha went down to the bottom of the ocean of existence to find those who had stayed too long or that were lost. If we can go back alone, that is great, but if we cannot, then these people are necessary. They are the shepherds who have been waiting for our safety. So when we go up we have to fight through the many levels of water. Because of the law of gravity and the water pressure, it is harder to go up. Plus we are tired, so to go up is harder than to go down. Now, if someone is beside us to show us the way with a torch and bring us new oxygen bottles, then we are safe and feel secure. You see, we do not belong to this world of existence, it is only for us to play in and explore for awhile. Because if we stay in the Kingdom of God for too long we might find it too blissful, or a little boring maybe!" [17]

"We are in the presence of God already. It is just that we do not recognize it, so we feel the burden of being separated, of being alone with all the pressures of this world. My intention is that you get a glimpse or some glimpses of this presence of God, and then you will be sure yourselves of His help, love and advice." [8]

Q. Chanting and praying are seen regularly in any temple or church. Are they the ways to reach enlightenment?

M. No. This is only a part of enlightenment. Praying and chanting is necessary to stimulate our sincerity and to create a
sincere and clean atmosphere. But we must be silent in
order to communicate with our silent God self. He is not
noisy. We are busy all day long speaking, thinking, and when
we go to the church we are busy again, talking and chanting,
telling God what to do. So when do you think that God has
time for us, or we have time for God? We have to sit in
silence or stand or lay in silence, and know where to find
God apart from prayers and chanting. [4]

Q. What do you think about the Old Testament and the Jewish religion?

M. It is good. But do not wait for the Messiah, because He comes
all the time. Pray that you recognize the present Messiah. The
one that you are waiting for will never come, if you expect
Him the way you do. Just like when Jesus came, people were
also expecting a Messiah and they killed the one at hand!

We do all the same stupid things. It isn't that the Jewish religion is bad, it is that we are ignorant. Even Jesus promised to
send us a comforter, that means someone that is equal to
Him, no? But two thousand years later, we are still waiting
and many prophets came and left the earth. We hear that
Jesus will reappear, right? How do you think He will look,
with wings, with a beard, or on a cross so that we may recognize Him? How could we recognize Him, if He would
come? We do not even know what Jesus looked like! We
weren't there, or maybe we were, but after two thousand
years who has such a big memory to remember!

Jesus comes not in appearance but in spirit. He can come to
anyone who is perceptive enough, who opens the right door
to let Him in. Then we become like Jesus, then He comes
back again. He comes whenever we are ready. He comes

through any Master who is capable to house His almighty power. That person is also Jesus, different hair style maybe, but it is still Jesus. [30]

Q. What is the relationship between our God nature and the seven chakras?

M. If you mean the bodily chakras up to here (Master points to her third eye) then there isn't any. I am talking above these chakras. Most of the yogis practicing on the chakras only stir up the heat motion. We have two currents in the body, one is the sound current, and the other the heat current. It takes care of the bodily motions, the digestion, the sweat, the blood circulation. The other current takes us back to the Kingdom of God. So when the yogis practice with the lower chakras (sexual, anus, solar plexus, throat chakra etc.) then there is no relationship, I only speak of the ones above these.[27]

Q. Why would God want Jesus to die the way He did?

M. Otherwise, His disciples would not be cleansed of their sins. The body of a Master is for two reasons. First, for the disciples in the physical world to be able to see. They couldn't see the astral body of the Master. Second, the body of a Master is for sacrifice. It is to receive all the things that the disciple has to get rid of, to deposit the sins of the disciples, and then to clean them out. [32]

Q. Could you tell us more about the true teachings of Jesus, compared with the Christian teachings of today?

M. Christ's teaching and the Christian teachings of today are both all right. Maybe the present teachings of Christianity are missing, have been censored in some parts, but this I dare not say in case I'll get in trouble. And the other teachings of Jesus, when He was alive, were more recorded. You see that in the Dead Sea Scrolls that I have read. They are supposed to be very ancient, even while Jesus was alive. Some things are missing in the Bible, but on the whole, the teachings of Christianity are okay. The only missing part is that Jesus is not here. That is the greatest missing part. So now we replace it with a direct line to Jesus. Should you want to see Him, you can see Him, you can talk to Him, you can learn directly from Him because He never dies. If the Church or any Christian organization can help you to get in touch with Jesus, and get a direct line to God's telephone number, then it is more correct, more fulfilling, more complete. If not, then we can supply this missing part for you, and that's all. Okay? [40]

Q. Did you know that Jesus was with the Essenes, a Holy Order which was by the Dead Sea?

M. Yes. He was from the Essenes' order, who were always vegetarians since thousands of years, and they had a lineage of transmission at that time. They were the 'White Brotherhood' who transmitted the light and the sound, and at that time it was very difficult to enter the order. You had to take vows of celibacy, and never to transmit the teaching outside openly. Anyone who entered the order had to be introduced by some elder members, and had to pass through many years of tests before they could wear the white robe. They were 'love incarnate' and Jesus was the one who broke the promise of keeping silent. But it was by the order of the Most High, of course. He got the inner message, otherwise, nobody in the Order had ever preached openly like this before. First, because of the vow. Second, because of the danger. Therefore, Jesus was crucified. He preached openly, and all the White Brotherhood were watching Him closely, trying to protect Him, in many ways. But they couldn't help it. [32]

4

Finding the Light

The Kingdom Within

"There is a better life, a more perfect life inside. Once we are perfect inside, our outside life will be perfect too. We can use our wisdom and power inside to make our work more efficient, faster and more beneficial to the world. So actually, if we want to be in any important position or to be successful in any field, we must get the proper power to work for us, not our minds. There are two levels of power: the first level, the power level, is the mind. The other higher level is all grace, love and miracles. By miracles, I don't mean changing the weather but we can do that too!" [26]

"Scientists have proven that we only use 5% of our brain. Fancy if we could use 100%! The one who can use 100% of his brain, that is a Christ, a Buddha, a Lao-tzu or whomever you believe is the greatest brain power in the world. They are the ones who know the secret access to the whole kingdom of our intelligence, what we call the Kingdom of God. Everything lays within ourselves. No one has been born without this Kingdom of God, just like the waves born from the ocean. Now, is there a way to gain control of this 100% of our intelligence? Yes, there are many ways, some take longer than others, some are more difficult than others. Some people do prayers, fasting, austerities. This we read in books of ancient wisdom, how people sacrificed everything to find God. But nowadays, if we follow this rigorous path, it is too hard, too time-consuming. We cannot just go in the jungle and leave society behind. In the ancient times, people had less desires and less comforts in life. Nowadays, we have more temptations due to comfort. They had less temptations and more free time to practice and find God." [18]

"How to find God? By reverting to the principles, that is, all loving, all forgiving, all compassion and all wisdom, by repenting our previous misdeeds committed through ignorance, and by resolving not to commit them again. With such a true repentance, the light of God will sprout forth again, and all our past sins will be forgiven. That is the true baptism; not by water, but by the Holy Spirit, by the light of wisdom and logic. That is why nowadays when we are baptized by water, we do not see any light from God, and we do not feel free of our sins, wisdom is not opened for us, and deep repentance is not evoked in our souls." [20]

"It is not as difficult to find God as it is to make money, I may tell you! When I was earning money, it was very difficult, working very hard 8 to 10 hours a day, and even that we squander away very fast. But if we are careful, we can make ends meet and save a little bit more for old age. But if we find the Kingdom of God, it lasts forever. Whatever intelligence, wisdom, happiness, joy we find, it will always be ours, never, ever will it be squandered away, never, ever can anyone steal it away from us." [18]

"Everyone has the inborn heaven, because the heaven is within us. Everyone has it and can find it. This I may assure you, that you may find it also, and immediately. The moment you want it you will get it, as quickly as that. But this nature has to be nourished every day, just like seeds need to be watered in order to grow. You can know your Buddha nature today, but you will become Buddha after some practice. Because we have been ignorant for so long, it takes a long, long time to wash out our habits, our lack of confidence in ourselves. We are used to people telling us what to do, that we are sinful, etc. After we get enlightened our head becomes clearer, we will experience how great we are, we will become more confident. We will know day after day with the practice of the Quan Yin Method that we are truly Christ, Christ-like or God-like, because God made man in His own image. He didn't make man to become a slave. We and God are made of the same essence, the only difference is whether or not we find it. God made everyone equally, some people found it and became great like Christ, like Buddha, and others have not found it and groveled in darkness life after life." [34]

Understanding God

"I have no intention to convince you that God exists. I am only among you to connect you with God, and then you will be able to believe me. I do not blame atheists because they do not see God inside of themselves. Not everyone can believe without proof. For those who do not believe in God, I offer them the opportunity to see Him through immediate enlightenment, so that you may discover your own nature, your own God-self." [15]

"You see, seeing is believing. God is too abstract, too intangible for us, if He is not brought down nearer to our understanding a little. How can He expect us to believe? This is blind faith. This is why I left to find enlightenment because I couldn't just read the Bible, read the scriptures, and say I believe Buddha, I believe God, basta, no! I had to have proof. I prayed to God every day. 'Please, if You exist, show me the way so I can find You, contact with You somehow. Open my eyes, open my ears, let me see, let me know at least Your love. Let me feel, let me know that You take care of us in some way or another.' So after enlightenment, after initiation you will feel every day that God is taking care of you. Truly that is so in all ways, in any situation, small things, big things. God does really take care and love us, and smoothes things out for us. He helps us in accidents, in sickness. He helps us in our dark days, helps us in every way. Then you may know that God truly exists. You will feel the overwhelming love power protecting and loving you. That is God. This is why people say God is love." [16]

"We have only to go upward to a higher and glorious world, to be near our Almighty God. The ocean of love and mercy is what we call God. He is not a being, although He might manifest Himself sometimes as a being to let us feel close, to be able to touch Him, and communicate with Him. Otherwise He is only an ocean of love and mercy and blessing and compassion. Everything that is good and joyous, that is God. We ourselves at the moment, even without initiation, without knowing our innate wisdom, our inborn heavenly power, we are still God.

Any time you manifest love toward your neighbor, toward your children, your friends, your relatives or anyone in need, you manifest God. Understand? So the more we manifest this kind of compassion, love, mercy and wisdom, the more we are near to God. But God in this sense is too limited. We can only help a handful of people at a time. God, in the ultimate sense, can help the whole world. So this is the goal we strive to achieve. This is what Buddha and Jesus achieved." [7]

"When the Buddha was alive, He told a story about four blind persons who touched an elephant and described it. The one who touched his ears said, 'Wow, an elephant is like a fan, a big fan,' and another one who touched his legs said, 'an elephant is like the pillar of a house,' and the other one who touched his nose said, 'the elephant looks like a water pipe, a hose,' and the one who touched his tail said, 'an elephant is like a broomstick,' (laughter). This is how we see God. This is how ordinary people see God, and this is how practitioners from different levels see God. Therefore, it is said that God is within you, Buddha is in your mind. That is the meaning of it." [34]

"In the universe, all things are created by energies, and we call that the creative force, or we might call it the Creator, because the energies have been scattered in all different directions in the universe, and have become different worlds and beings. And now, these beings have acquired an individual state of thinking, or level of consciousness, and according to the interaction between each other, they will generate another kind of energy. We will divide it into two categories. The first one, we can call positive energy or God nature, heavenly force or Buddha nature. The second category, we can call negative nature, evil or dark force, or the opposite of goodness.

Now the goodness and the positive energy are side by side with the negative energies. Whenever any being, be they angels or earth people, whenever they generate goodness, tolerance, love, compassion and cooperation with each other, then these energies will be categorized as good or God force, positive power. The more beings generate this kind of goodness, the more positive power we have in the atmosphere or in our world. And whenever we or any beings generate hatred, bad thoughts, or any kind of negative tendencies, actions or speech, we add more into the negative storehouse of the atmosphere. That we call evil. And this force will reap more hatred, more wars, more disharmony in our world, or any world that these people happen to reside in." [36]

"It is like electricity, there are two poles, one negative and the other positive, and when the plus and minus are put together it creates power. But actually electricity is neither positive nor negative, but without positivity and negativity, we have no electricity. So it is the same with all things. God is neither good nor bad. He is only an ocean of indifference and love. He knows no hatred, no dirtiness, no bad and no sin; He discriminates not between bad and good, beautiful and ugly. So we call Him the Ocean of Love and Mercy." [5]

Q. When you describe God, you use the masculine word "He." Is God masculine, feminine, both or neither?

M. Both. Neither. Okay, then I'll use She! Because if I use She maybe you will also object. Since ancient times, we have always referred to God as He, and now who are you to say that God is a She! I just comply to your own customs and understanding about God. I dare not make too much revolution. I am afraid you may scold me for changing God's sex! [14]

Q. What is God? Does It have a form or look like paintings of God that we see?

M. Like Michelangelo's God? No, this is his God, it is Michelangelo's God. You want to see what God looks like? Who is it who asked this question? Please raise your hand. I will show you immediately. You? Look behind you, your neighbor in front, to your right and left, that is what God looks like. Alright, you are satisfied? God said, *"God made man in His own image,"[1]* so if you want to find God, look at your neighbors. Each one of us houses God inside. So see through the physical wall and then you will find God in yourself and in each other. So treat each other as God, and then you will see how much different life is day after day. [41]

Q. How can I express my God light?

M. You can only express it when you have it. So have God's light first. After initiation, then you can express it. We can't show our money when we do not know where the money is, right? Even if we have it, we must know where it is, in order to show it to people. So even if you have God's light within you, you must know it first, contact it first, and then you can show it to people. I can show you the light because I have the light. I am in possession of the light. I know I have it. You have it, but you don't know. That's the difference between us. [40]

Enlightenment or the Great Awakening

"Enlightenment is the process of knowing what is greater than life, what is greater than the things we can see with our physical eyes, or touch with our physical instruments. It is the moment when we begin to know something greater than that, the true governor of the whole universe, which is also within ourselves.

Enlightenment means inner awakening. You realize that you have a power that is much greater than what you use every day. Usually, we follow the directions of our ego, but after enlightenment, we follow God's will. We are connected with Him and recognize our real value. But at the same time we become very

1 Genesis 1:26

humble. The more we know about ourselves the more humble we become. We know that there is a greater force in the universe, and it isn't for our human understanding to discuss and to grasp. So we become humble and then very powerful, because we have a higher power within us, and use it every day for the benefit of others. As we tap within ourselves into the right source of positive power, which is called in Christian terminology, 'the spirit that dwells within you,' or God Almighty, we open that source that was closed before. So once that source is opened we become powerful like Christ, like Buddha. We can help many people with this inborn God power, and then we become more humble because we see within everyone the same power, so we respect everyone as living God." [53]

"Enlightenment is a gift from God, and not the result of virtuous or charitable deeds. We can all become enlightened or liberated. If not, why would God have sent Jesus or Buddha or Mohammed if we were so helpless, if only the virtuous souls could achieve it? And I do not know who is really virtuous because, 'Every saint has a past and every sinner has a future.' We are not such sinners. It is an illusion and after you understand this, you will know that there isn't any virtue or sin. We must however work a great deal to realize this. The Quan Yin Method offers you a method free of charge to rediscover your original purity and noble heritage." [35]

"When I experienced the great awakening, I saw that I was in every creature and enjoyed whatever it was in that particular situation, be it a butterfly, a bird or an angel, a rock or a tree, everything was as perfect as it is. It is hard to explain it in words, but ultimately all of us will reach that kind of understanding if we yearn for it, and then we will know for ourselves. This is the only way for us to end our illusion, our belief about this ephemeral existence. When we see through our human understanding, everything looks dif-

ferent, but when we are in a higher state of consciousness everything is more joyous, light-hearted and positive." [18]

"Only when we are truly enlightened can we enjoy anything.
Whatever comes, we can enjoy. When good things come, we take
them as a gift from God, wholeheartedly, without any guilt or
reservation, without any obstacles whatsoever in our heart or in
our thinking, because the nature of an enlightened person is very
free, very carefree, very easy, just like a child. If you give him
something good, he accepts it, he won't think that you want to
trick him, or whether he deserves it or not, he just accepts it.
And, when the circumstances do not allow that we have comfort
or richness in life, then we are also happy to carry on that way,
we have no desire for material greatness. But this doesn't mean
that we don't strive to work for the society, and that we don't do
our best to fulfill our obligations as a citizen of the world. We do,
all the same, we do more effectively and with all willingness to
contribute our part to the whole world. The difference is that we
do without a desire for reward or praise. Should we fail or should
people misunderstand our goodwill, we still can bear it, we will
not have any suffering in our heart." [19]

The Three Ways to Obtain Spiritual Liberation

"We have three ways to become liberated. I have talked
about the devotional way, which is the easiest. You just believe in
a saint and pray to Him or Her for blessings and deliverance,
and when you leave this world you will be liberated. The second
is, you get initiation from a Master and become a Master yourself. This is of course more ideal, because then you can also save
your family and other beings, not only yourself. It is more
noble, and is what God wants or the Master wants from us.

When a person becomes a Master, he can save numerous beings from heaven to hell; he can save any beings, and walk on any kind of plane. The third way to be saved is by being a relative or a friend of an initiated person, even if you are already dead. If you were dead, already in hell, and suppose your great, granddaughter is initiated by a great Master, then you would immediately be free and go to heaven. If we are a friend of an initiated person, then we will also get help from the Master.

These are the three ways to liberation. Of course I emphasize the way of self-discipline, because once we are initiated and start on the path of self-discipline toward self-realization, then our many, many generations (past, present and future) will also get liberation. It is because these generations and relatives have been connected to us by the 'Law of Karma,' which means give and take, cause and effect, which carries on for many lives and many generations." [12]

Q. Once the soul is awakened, does it stay actively awake?

M. Yes, always. The body will sleep, the mind will get sometimes entangled in other purposes, but the soul never does it again. Once awakened, it is always awakened. But even then, we need a cooperative mind, body and emotions in order to work best, to benefit the world more, with the soul's directing power. Therefore, after initiation, even when we have a taste of enlightenment, and know ourselves, we still continue with our training, in order to make the mind used to the enlightened way of the soul, and not to sink down again in the physical level, and the worn out conceptions and habit-forming ways of doing things. [27]

Immediate Enlightenment

"Immediate enlightenment means to be enlightened right away. At that moment, one begins to sit down to face the Supreme Master inside oneself. This is the true self. This self truly belongs to you, and you had it before you were born, before you were absorbed in greed, hatred or lust. This self is truly your Supreme Master. When you descend here you should open your mind and listen to what He teaches you, then you will be enlightened immediately. Therefore, there is no need for it to be written down, nor for instruction." [57]

"It is not easy to bring home these abstract ideas with simple and ordinary words, but when we understand that it is deep inside us, and part of ourselves, then we feel very easy and very elated. But this is one of the intellectual enlightenments only. In Zen meditation, sometimes they call it Sudden Enlightenment or Immediate Enlightenment, because one word from the teacher sets you free in some parts, or maybe sets you free a great deal, or completely.

But then again, why do we have to meditate after enlightenment, or after we already understood what the Master or the teacher wanted to say? It is because we have too many habits, too much knowledge, because one time is not enough to convince us that we are enlightened. We probably will forget it the next day. So we should repeat these experiences of enlightenment until our mind accepts it. It is not enough for the Self to recognize itself, because the Self has always known the Self anyhow. But because we are in this world, we have to do everything with the instrument that is the mind, the computer. That is the tool that we have to use to work in this world, to bring the blessing and power of love into the chaotic environment, in order to make a better world for our children to come." [49]

Q. The initiation periods in ancient Egypt, for instance, were at least 7 years. Usually initiation is regarded as a rather long process by which one earns enlightenment. It seems to suit our modern life to say "You can now be enlightened!" I wonder how is this so?

M. In ancient times, it was not easy to find a Master even. And if you had found one he would test you for long years, very long, like Milarepa of Tibet. He was tested for 4 years with a lot of scolding and beating sometimes. But today, if you do that, the Master will be put in jail! (laughter) It is not allowed anymore, and besides with our world's very fast and advanced way of life, we can't just cling onto this kind of method of testing disciples. Today we have to tune in with the modern pace of the society. Of course, it makes more troubles for the teacher, because he doesn't have time to ground the disciple, to make him earn what is very precious. But what do you think, if a Master does that? How much longer before he will be enlightened? It takes a long time. You see, the enlightenment is very fast, but the process of seven years is to test the disciple, and to ground him into moral discipline. This is very good also, but because of that, in ancient times, not many people were enlightened. Because of ignorance, they crucified Jesus, because not many people knew what enlightenment was, and what meditation practice was, it was so new and so strange. Therefore, today many Masters make it open to the public as a sacrifice of the Master's time, expense and a lot of efforts to bring their disciples into a fast moral standard, and a very high level of enlightenment. It is a different time, and enlightenment doesn't mean that you are completely enlightened. You have a taste of enlightenment so you are encouraged to go further with it. In the old times, the Masters didn't do this. They would let you work first and really suffer for it and you would appreciate it more." [48]

Q. It is said that the enlightened soul doesn't think or act, he is only an observer and doesn't make decisions. How can we live in this world without acting or choosing? It is also said that to act is to disturb the order of nature, and to compensate for this imbalance, nature will create some opposition. Do you agree with this?

M. Well, you must first be enlightened, and then you will know what happens! To act without acting doesn't mean that you are lifeless, mindless, without a soul, but that you are simply doing everything naturally. It is true that you no longer have to make decisions, you only act according to God's will and you know exactly what to do. Even if from the outside, you seem to act like everyone else, it isn't the case because all your acts are dictated by God. You no longer have responsibilities and you always act for the best. But this doesn't mean that anyone behaving without thinking is acting God's will, because he doesn't know His will. After enlightenment we know the original Plan and act accordingly. Before being enlightened, we only disturb it by trying to force our will over the Divine Plan. [18]

Q. How many levels of consciousness are there and how can you find which one you are on?

M. Before we reach the highest level of Truth, we have to go through five levels of consciousness. We can know this by recognizing the light, the intensity of the light we see inside, and also the scenery, the heavenly abode we see inside and that we can recognize. Another way of recognizing is through the sound. Each level of consciousness vibrates at a different rate and by knowing which sound corresponds to which level, we can know more or less our own achievement. But after some time, you become expert, and you will know immediately someone's level. We can judge our level of inner achievement by our own outward actions, like becoming more loving, more tolerant, more dedicated to the whole of mankind." [63]

Beyond This World

"Beyond our world, there are many different worlds. Each level is a world in itself, and it represents our level of understanding. It's just like when we go into a university. Each grade, as we go through the university, represents our understanding more about the university's teaching, and then we slowly move toward graduation. In the astral world, we will see many kinds of so-called miracles. We can heal the sick. We can sometimes see something that other people cannot see. We have at least six kinds of miraculous powers. We can see beyond the ordinary boundary, we can hear beyond the limits of space. The distance doesn't make a difference to us. That's what we call the heavenly ears and the heavenly eyes. We can also see through people's thinking, what they have in their mind, etc. These are the powers that sometimes we acquire when we have access to the first level of the Kingdom of God.

Now, if we go a little bit beyond this level to what we call the second world, just for the sake of simplifying matters, then we will probably have a lot more abilities than the first one, including miracles. But the most striking achievement we can have at the second level is that of eloquence of speech and the ability to debate. No one seems to be able to conquer a person who has achieved the second level because he has tremendous power of eloquence, and his intellect is at the peak of his power.

Most of the people who have an ordinary mind or very simple IQ cannot match this person because his IQ has opened to a very high degree. It is not only the physical brain that has been developed more, it is the mystical power, it is the heavenly power, the wisdom that is inherent inside us. Now it begins to open. In India, people call this level 'Buddhi,' which means intellectual level. When you achieve 'Buddhi,' you become a Buddha.

That's where the word Buddha came from. The Buddha is precisely just that. It's not finished. There is more than that. Most people call an enlightened person a Buddha. If he doesn't know beyond the second level, he would probably feel very proud about it. Yes, thinking that he is a living Buddha and his disciples would be very proud calling him Buddha. But actually if he only achieves the second level in which he can see through the past, present and future of any person he chooses to see, and in which he has an absolute eloquence of speech, then it's not yet the end of the Kingdom of God.

Every so-called miracle would happen to us, whether we want it or not, because our intellect just opened and just knows how to contact the higher source of healing, of arranging everything so that our life would become smoother and better.

The so-called third world is a higher step. The one who goes to the third world has to be absolutely clean of every debt of this world, at least. If we owe something to the king of this physical world, we cannot go up. Just like if you are a criminal of some nation and your record is not clear, you cannot pass beyond the border to go to another nation. So, the debt of this world includes many things that we've done in the past, and in the present, and maybe in the future days of our physical life. Now all these have to be cleared, the so-called karma.

Now, suppose you have passed the third world, what next? Of course, you go to the next higher level, the fourth. The fourth world is already out of extraordinary. We cannot just use the simple language to describe all these things to the lay person for fear of offending the Lord of that world. Because that world is so beautiful even though there are some parts of it that are very dark, darker than on a black-out night in New York. Before you reach the light, it's darker than that. It's kind of a forbidden city.

Before we reach God's knowledge, we are stopped over there. But with a Master, with an experienced Master, you can pass through. Otherwise, we cannot find the road in that kind of world.

When we reach different levels, or planes of existence, we have experienced not only spiritual changes, but physical and intellectual changes with everything else in our life. We look at life in a different manner, we walk differently, we work differently. Even our daily work takes on a different meaning, and we understand why we work this way, why we have to be in this job, or why we should change this job. We understand our purpose of life, so we no longer feel restless and agitated. But we wait very harmoniously, patiently for our mission on earth to finish, because we know where we are going next. We know while we are living.

So after that you go to a higher level. After the fourth, you go to the next higher level. The house of the Master which is the fifth level. All the Masters came from there. Even though their levels are higher than the fifth, they stay there. It is the residence of the Master. Beyond that, there are many aspects of God, which are difficult to understand. After the fifth, you can go anywhere you want.

There are many more levels upward, but it is more comfortable, more neutral to stay there. It is too powerful, further upward. You can go for awhile, but maybe you wouldn't like to rest there.

There are many aspects of God that we could not imagine. We always imagine the higher we go, the more loving. But there are different kinds of love. There is violent love, strong love, mild love, neutral love. So it depends on how much we can bear, God will give us different degrees of love from God. But sometimes it is strong, we feel we are torn into ribbons." [38]

5

What is Meant by Masters

"Masters are those who remember their origin and, out of love, share this knowledge with whomever seeks it, and take no pay for their work. They offer all their time, finance and energy to the world. When we reach this level of mastership, not only do we know our origin, but we can also help others to know their true worth. Those who follow the direction of a Master, quickly find themselves in a new world, full of true knowledge, true beauty and true virtues. All beauty, knowledge and virtue in the outside world is there to remind us of the true world inside. The shadow, however beautiful, is never as good as the real object itself. Only the real thing can satisfy our soul, which is the Master of the house." [52]

"A Master is supposed to be the one who has already realized Himself and who knows what His or Her real self is. Therefore, He is able to communicate with God, the greatest intelligence, because it is within ourselves. That is why He or

She can transmit this knowledge, this awakening power to whomever would like to share the joy.

Actually, we don't have a Master in a sense. Only until the disciple is able to recognize his own mastership, then a so-called Master is necessary to guide him until then only. But we don't have a contract or anything. Of course, you have a contract with yourself that you should stick to the end, and this is for your own benefit. And initiation just means the moment of first recognition of your greater spirit, that's it." [53]

"While a living Master is on earth he takes on some of the karma of the people, especially those who believe in the Master, and even more-so those who are disciples of the Master. And this karma has to be worked out. Therefore, the Master suffers for the disciples, and for mankind at large, in his lifetime. And it is manifested through his body. Therefore, he might be sick, he might be ill, he might be tortured, he might be nailed on the cross, or he might be slandered. Any Master has to go through this kind of thing. You can see it for yourself, even Buddha, Mohammed, Christ and many other Masters in the East or West. No one has ever lived their life peacefully without persecution. That is what is meant by a Master sacrificing for mankind. But only as long as He has the body to suffer the karma, because karma in this world is physical. If you want to save people out of the physical karma, you need a physical body. Therefore, a Master has to manifest a physical body to take on all the troubles and sufferings." [24]

"A Master is in the world to help those who need help. But then, He is not in the world, He is not attracted to the world, He is not attached to the world, nor is He attached to his failure or success in this world. You saw what Jesus did at the peak of His glory. He was ready to die if it should be so. By dying, He taught many people the way of surrendering. By not clinging to glory and life, He taught God's will. He taught that we should always follow God's will." [27]

How Do We Recognize a Real Master?

"It is very easy! First of all, a real Master will not accept any donations for His or Her own use, because God only gives and never takes. Second, He or She must give you some proof of enlightenment. For example, if someone proclaims to have light, then He must also give you some light or give you the proof that you can hear the Word of God. Whomever can give you a proof of the light and the Word of God, that is someone you can believe. Guru means light-giver, darkness-remover. Otherwise, how would you know if He has anything to offer?" [4]

"A false master will always advertise his little miracles, but a real Master will never do so. If He is forced to, He will always act in secret. The disciple only will know, and only when it is necessary, to save him from a dangerous situation, to cure his illness, to help him mentally or to accelerate his spiritual progress. The disciple will then know the value of his Master. A real Master can only give and not take. His disciples are comfortable but the Master has to suffer. That is why it is said that Jesus had to uplift mankind and that He had to be crucified. He couldn't enjoy any privilege. That is why people scolded Him and crucified Him. Anyhow, once you learn this method, you are protected 100% by God's power. The Master alone has to endure all kinds of suffering so everyone can enjoy. But this is the joy of being a parent! The children enjoy all the comforts and the parents have to work to provide all the things, and take all the responsibilities." [4]

"A real Master never has selfish motives. His heart and mind are entirely devoted to the well-being of others. Whenever a Master is on earth, He takes on some of the karma of the people, those who believe in Him and especially His disciples. Now, their karma has to be worked out, so the Master has to suffer for His disciples and for mankind at large, in His lifetime and this is manifested through His body. Therefore, He might be sick, tortured, nailed to a cross, slandered and persecuted. Every Master has to go through this." [64]

Q. How does one recognize his or her Master? Can an individual have more than one living Master?

M. I think that one is enough. If you learn with one Master, you already have a lot to learn, how would you learn with two or three? You couldn't even catch up, never mind learn with two. There are different degrees of Masters, but you must know and pray for the highest, the best, so that you may be liberated in one life. Otherwise, it takes a long time. Yes, you can make it in two, three lives or in two or three thousand years. So pray for the best and get only the best, that would be the best! And if you are sincere in your prayer, God will send you only the best. Ask for the best, that is, to only want to know God in this lifetime, to send you someone who can help you know God. Otherwise, He will send you someone who can take you to some heavens, or can give you some magical powers, this kind of fancy stuff! But if you pray to know God, and God alone, in one lifetime, He will send you the best, the fastest, the most powerful. [30]

Q. Master, were Hermes, Zoroaster, the Essenes, and the Gnostics Masters? Who were the first Masters? And what is the Great White Brotherhood?

M. All true Masters are one. All came from one source, and the highest Master is the Supreme Master, the Almighty, which is in all of you. When we first came here, we were Masters. We blessed the world and forgot all about our power and glory, and our energy was exhausted because we paid attention to outer phenomena. So all the Masters who came here are the ones who are awakened in this awareness. They know their true glory and can travel the road home frequently, and they can lead us home. So, no need to discriminate between Masters. All the religions are founded after the Master has gone. Therefore, we have Christians after Christ, Buddhists after Buddha, etc." [45]

The Three Types of Masters

"It is easy to find a Master if we know that there are different types, and know which type is most suitable for us. In my opinion there are three types of Masters. The first type is what we call the intellectual type, the scholars. They are very knowledgeable about scriptures, versed in the terminology within the realm of philosophy. They can teach you who wrote what scripture when, and the meaning of its terminology. These teachers are very worthy of our reverence. They can transmit to us some of the holy teaching from the ancient times that we may not have the time to understand, or maybe that we are not expert enough to know the terminology. That is the first type of teacher. Learning with them about different teachings and religions, our knowledge will be broadened.

The second type of teachers are absorbed in ecstasy or Samadhi all the time. They are entirely devoted to God, to the Holy Plan. They are in direct contact with God and have direct knowledge from God. They can see Him face to face. And if we are in contact with these Masters by chance, or by our own will, we will derive some benefits. Our mundane mind will be less burdened by the pressure of the world, and we will feel uplifted and happy and regain a longing for God. We will feel like we want to renounce the world. I don't mean by that to shave your head and live in the jungle, but to feel less desire for the sensual pleasures and the material gain of this world. These teachers are usually hard to find, because they mostly do not really teach, they just absorb themselves in ecstasy, enjoying the bliss and harmony within.

The third type also absorb themselves in the love for God, but they also have love and compassion for those who are in ignorance and suffering. Therefore, they run around as per request. Even if there was only one or two people sincerely longing to be reunited with God, they would come and share with them the secret of the Kingdom of God, the way to find the Reality, the Truth, the Tao within ourselves, of how to awaken within them the greatest source of knowledge, of all power and saving power within ourselves, in order to lessen the intensity of suffering in our lives, in order to develop our own self-confidence and merge with the almighty source from which we come.

This is a basic outline of the three types of teachers. So, we have to look for one type that could satisfy our desire, needs and inner longing. If we happen to see any Master, then we must use our discrimination to see whether this is the Master we want, whether he or she is worthy of our reverence and trust.

The first type of teacher is easy to recognize because of his erudition. He can talk and know all the scriptures, and we know he is a man of knowledge. It is easy to know this, because worldly knowledge is easy to understand and to test. The second type is also easy to recognize by their appearance and the devotional atmosphere around people always absorbed in ecstasy. The third type of Master is difficult to detect because when a person is not in ecstasy, it is difficult to know if He has ever been in ecstasy or not, because this type of teacher is 24 hours a day in an invisible 'Samadhi' or ecstasy. Samadhi means that you are in ecstasy, in bliss, tranquility and light.

You can be in ecstasy while living in this world. There are two kinds of Samadhi: One is after you leave this world, you are forever in ecstasy, in bliss, in the Kingdom of God. You are one with God or the Ocean of Love and Mercy. The other type is a smaller ecstasy that you experience every day through meditation, through devotional longing, or any type of ritual in order to reach ecstasy. So when you are in Samadhi, you forget the whole world. Sometimes you can hear the people around you, but cannot relate to the world. When you are in a deeper ecstasy, the whole world disappears, and you only see light and God, and feel peace, bliss and ecstasy.

Because the third type of Masters are in and out of ecstasy at the same time, like Jesus or Buddha, it is difficult to detect them. They look like ordinary people. This is the danger of being a third degree Master. The first kind of teacher, everybody knows you, reveres you, thousands of people follow you. The second type of teacher, everyone knows and bows to their feet. You may know it or not because you are in ecstasy all the time and people can see. But the third type, like Jesus or Buddha, people may throw stones at them, nail them, scold them and kill them, because many people could not believe that they are the sons of God, that they are the Salvation, the Light and the Way of the world, when they are in the physical body and acting like most ordinary men.

So, those who go around and share their secret of the Kingdom of God to people, like Jesus or Buddha did, are in ecstasy and out of ecstasy. Because, when you are preaching, your real Self is in Samadhi, but your physical self still suffers, still knows pain and sorrow. Now, the second type of Masters feel no pain in their bodies, no worry, no anxiety, only bliss, all the misery disappears, and there is no word in this language to describe this state. If you belong to the first and second category, people will recognize you and follow you. But the danger in being a Master of the third type is that they look like ordinary people, and people might throw stones at them, even kill them because they don't believe that they are the way to salvation." [16]

Why We Need a Living Master

"Love and respect we must have for any great person, for any great soul, any great practitioners like Jesus or Buddha, those great beings who sacrificed so much for mankind and who have reached their ultimate Wisdom. Love and respect we must always have, even if that person has passed away. But then, we don't need to devote all our time just to praise them, to worship them and to ask favors from them. Because any person would know that we are living beings, and we need a living Master in order to impart us the knowledge that the past teachers have given to their past disciples. So a living Master we must find.

Anyhow, past Masters, even if you love and worship them, can only help you to a certain extent because they have left our magnetic field. They have gone to another world, to another kind of dimension to work in their present work, and they are busy over there. So, a living Master is the one who is assigned to do their past work in the present time. It is just like when Mr.

Carter was President some years ago, but now it is Mr. Bush. So it is no good to worship and call Mr. Carter to solve your national problems when he is no longer in office. It is not that we don't like him, or respect his work, or appreciate his job, but he is gone now. We have to leave him so he can do his job and we have to request the person who is presently occupying his position, to fulfill his job for us. That's all." [33]

"Once you leave this physical world, even if you are a very high Master, you cannot help the physical beings any more, but only through an inner communication, which is very difficult to reach for most human beings, save some exceptional persons who have the inborn nature of telepathy, or who are left with some psychic power, or the inner communication ability, through their own previous lives' practice. We might call this the sixth and seven sense, the highest dimension of understanding. Then, you may even be able to see Jesus without practicing or any prior meditation. It has happened, but not very often." [5]

"In your meditation, if you run into any difficulty or if you have any questions, you should pray to God, and try to quiet your mind, and the answer will come or the help will come. Or pray to Jesus or pray to Buddha, or whichever saint you believe in. Our teachings are universal, we have no discrimination between belief systems. Then, I have to add that, if after you have prayed to all the saints, and to God and it doesn't help, then you can call me to help you. It sounds very self-glorifying, but I tell you because I have to tell you everything, and I have to explain why it is so. It is because I am nearer. A nearer neighbor is better than a far relative. It is very simple and logical. I am nearer because we are in the same magnetic field of the earth. Our energy is intertwined and it is easier to oscillate our energies because we are nearer, we are in the same vibratory frequency." [56]

"When you have a living Master, you can pray in silence, and ask him for advice if you encounter problems with your meditation. If you feel far away from God, you will need an intermediary. You are still a little weak, just like a child needing the help of his parents to guide his first steps. But later on, you will walk all alone, and know that your goal is to walk alone, and no longer depend on your parents. You will be able to learn directly from the Masters of the past with the Quan Yin Method. That is how we learn about the Truth, not from hearsay, from sermons or doctrines. The Truth is revealed through our own intuition. When we reach higher dimensions, we discover other beings and a more 'civilized' universe that can only be perceived by concentrating our attention within ourselves, and by reaching a level of deep contemplation. The Quan Yin Method is a way to achieve this state." [22]

"Past Masters cannot teach you. You have to look for a present Master, who can answer your questions, help you when you are in doubt, and take you by the hand back to the Kingdom of God. We need a person-to-person contact, not someone from the past. It doesn't matter how beautiful a woman was in the past, you cannot marry her! She cannot give you any children and produce the love feeling that you have with a living wife." [55]

"A living Master is useful. I have electricity. A dead wire doesn't work, only a living wire can conduct electricity and bring it to you. Any wires, no matter how powerful, if they have been destroyed, cannot carry any more electricity. Any bulb, no matter how beautiful, once it is broken, cannot give you light. But a bulb, even an ugly one, if it is intact, can give you light. That is why, when people pray to a dead Buddha, they will rarely get a response." [21]

Master offers her love and blessing by sharing candies with the gathered initiates.

Master spends an intimate moment with new initiates in Mexico.

Master patiently answers the earnest questions of disciples.

A model of humility and unconditional love.

Master provides inspiration through storytelling.

"Through your thinking of the Master, you become one with the Master, and the Master is you. The Master is your own real Self, but since you do not realize it, you just have to think of the Master because that is yourself. Through the thinking, all the qualities of the Master gradually, by and by, will transmit to you, and you will find your Self through the Master. And later, you will realize, 'Oh! Master is me. It was me all the time.' That is why, since ancient times, people worship sages and enlightened Masters, for themselves, not for the sake of the Master." [66]

Q. So, what it sounds like to me, is that until you can find the Master within yourself, you'll need to have one outside for a while?

M. But the Master is also an inner guide, not only on the physical level. Otherwise, the Master wouldn't be able to help the disciple from a thousand miles away, and all over the world. The Master must be at a very elevated level in order to help all the people anytime, day and night, no matter where the person is.

Q. In the West, there is often a danger when a seeker falls down and adores the teacher. Do you think this is a problem?

M. Not if the teacher is genuine, because then you only worship yourself, you only worship the greatest spirit which is already one with the Master.

Q. So you are saying that if the Master is a genuine Master, He or She then holds a mirror up to the person to help them see themselves deeply?

M. Right, that's it. [53]

Q. What about the disciples of previous Masters? If a true living Master leaves this world, do His disciples have to seek another Master, or is there no need for that?

M. No need. But if they want to inquire something about practical things, or physical things, then they could come to another living Master, or to the successor of that Master. Otherwise, inside, there is still the spiritual guidance of the deceased Master. He is still responsible and still has the power to carry on, because the connection is already made. You understand? Only when we don't have a so-called connection with a past Master do we need a new Master. Why we didn't go to a past Master from many hundreds of years ago was because we didn't make a connection with Him while He was living, therefore the connection was not made. If you have made a connection with a Master a thousand years ago, it doesn't matter how long it has been, He still takes care of you. But if you didn't make a connection with Him before He died, then how can he take care of you? Do you understand? [33]

Q. So what would you like to say about yourself in relationship to what you can offer people?

M. I myself couldn't offer much except for my body, speech and mind whenever God wills to use it to offer it to people, to His children who love to be near Him, or to be next to Him. I can only be ready to be used. I cannot offer anything much. (laughter) I am only like you. What can a body offer? [22]

Q. Could you perform some miracles so people can increase their faith in your teaching?

M. Miracles, what do you want? I give you some money, yes? And then what do you do with it? What good would that do to you eternally? I advise you to find your own power, your own miraculous power, instead of relying on mine, instead of coming to me only for magical powers, in order to get your own right back, the Kingdom of God, your own wisdom, your own birthright, your own heaven, your own Kingdom. That is the best and the highest ideal of a human life, not miracles. Miracles are very short-lived.

> If necessary I will show you miracles, but not for show, not to get your applause. Whenever necessary during your practice, you may encounter some obstacles, some bad influence. At that time you will know that I can make miracles. I can, but I do not use them at random just to let you know how great I am. I do not need that. I want you to have a very correct attitude, correct thinking, a correct idea in practice and that is to go back to the most high, to gain back our highest wisdom, not to hang on to these children's games, to these plastic toys. You will have everything, *'Seek ye first the Kingdom of God and all other things will be added unto you.'* [1] Do not ask for small things, ask for great things. It befits you more because we human beings are the greatest in the universe. So ask for the greatest only, that is most befitting to your position, to your dignity and to your birthright. [14]

Q. Master, you travel all around the world and cannot stay here to teach everyone, so in your absence who will we have to follow?

M. It is like this. We do not follow a teacher, we only follow the teaching. So we can never go wrong, in case the teacher goes wrong. When the teaching is okay, then we follow the teaching. We have to see if the teaching is correct. You see if my ethics are correct or not, if whatever I teach you I follow or not. For example, I teach you not to eat meat and I also eat vegetarian. I teach you not to steal and I also do not steal. I teach you to give away in charity and I myself give away in charity. I teach you to love people and I do love people and help people. I take no money for the teaching I give, I earn my own money, so you have nothing to lose at all. You can only gain.

1 Matthew 6:33

Now also, every moral standard described in the Buddhist scriptures, and in the Christian Bible, I convey to you again. So, I teach nothing new, nothing immoral, nothing unethical. Do you understand? So you may be safe to know that your teacher won't teach you anything amoral or unethical, anything outside of the scriptures. I teach you everything from the scriptures. From ancient times, the ethical conduct hasn't changed, the commandments from God and from Buddha have not changed. I teach you the same, and I do the same, so you know at least that I am not a bad type! So now the teaching is correct, right?

And the meditation will provide you with wisdom and peace of mind. It doesn't matter which technique, it will help you somewhat. So there is no exception about our technique. I only tell you that it is the fastest, that is all. You don't have to believe me. I only inform you and now you have your own choice. I only tell the truth. If it is fast, I say it is very fast. I am also a nun. I am not allowed to say lies. Even average people don't tell lies, so what would a nun tell lies for? And I have no reason to do this, because I don't need your money. I don't need anything, and I do not even live here. I profit nothing from you. I may even leave tomorrow and you may never see me again. Good-bye! So I have profited nothing. So from this standpoint you are safe. Yes?

So, you follow the teaching, don't follow me. The teaching will always be with you, and you do not need to follow me in person. In case you want some personal advice about your meditation progress, you may write to me or you may telephone to ask me. Nowadays no need to stick with the Master, you can go to Taiwan or wherever I stay. My body is only an appearance, a house, an office so that you may see me. If I were to only use my spiritual body, you couldn't see me at all, you couldn't hear me. So how could I convey the message to you? So I have to use my body, right? So, no need to fear that when I go away, you will have no one. You always have someone. You might even see me appear in your house, just like this, if you are sincere and high level enough. You will see the Master come to you, and you will see the Master all the time when you need. No need to cling to the physical body." [14]

Q. Master, as your disciple, if I have a friend or someone I know that is very sick, and if I ask you to help this person, could you help this person, or can you only help someone who follows your teaching?

M. The Master helps anyone that is dear to you, but according to his karma and what is good for him also. Ask anyhow, but offer the result to the Master's power. [47]

The Love for a Living Master

"The love for the Master never changes, it just develops. First, you love the physical presence of the Master and later you love everyone, even without their presence. You will feel more tolerant, more loving, unconditionally. You will love without knowing you love. It will be very natural, very comfortable. What you love, is the love for me. You feel free, more developed, more loved in the presence of a Master. You feel more self-confident and self-worth. You know that this person will never harm you, will only help you to develop your self-worth, and never ask anything in return. This is the only love that can move every heart. It never fades, even from one life to the next. Once you are initiated, it is forever. Everywhere you go, you feel that love with you. So, you are happy to be around it, just like the moths, they like to be near the light.

Everybody likes the invisible great light of a Master, because this light has everything we need for our thirsty soul, everything that the world cannot satisfy. So to get satisfaction, you sit next to the Master. You don't love the appearance of the Master, but the inner beauty.

When you think of me you smile, no? You feel happy, a kind of bliss. But the worldly love will always bind you to this world. If you are bound to me, you go where I go, but if you are bound to someone else, you go where they go.(laughter) Sometimes it leads you to misery, hatred, jealousy and to all kinds of bondage. But the love for the Master is different. The more you love the Master, the more freedom you get, all kinds of freedom in aspects you never knew before, because you were bound by society, conceptions, customs, family ties. Now, nothing can bind you, no desires, no habits, no kind of lower desires. That is the difference between noble love, and the lower desire which we call love, and which is karma binding. You love me, but you can leave me anytime. That's the difference, you don't need to fear." [21]

The Path of The Great Masters

"Our world is better now compared to the old times because many Masters have stepped down to earth and taught many great laws of civilization. We have improved. That is why our world has become more civilized, more bright, more comfortable compared to thousands of years ago. This is due to many, many great enlightened Masters who have elevated our understanding. Even though they taught just a group of people, but the teachings that they left behind, the vibration and the seeds continue to grow and benefit the whole world on a large scale, and have lifted up the whole consciousness of mankind to a higher level. Therefore, our world is getting better and better every day." [26]

"When a Master comes to the earth, not only the disciples are uplifted and shown the wisdom, but the whole of mankind will also be purified and uplifted to a higher level of consciousness. Therefore, many Masters have graced our earth, and the world has become better, as it is today. But even then, it has not reached the level of the heavenly understanding. It has not reached the same consciousness like many other worlds in the universe." [32]

"If we want to reach the same heights as the ancient Masters, we have to follow the same path they took. It is so simple. It is just like if you want to become a doctor, you have to attend a university, and follow the curriculum. The graduated doctors will teach you how to become one. Similarly, to become Christ-like, we must practice their method, we have to contact the inner light and Word of God. And I can offer you this method, freely, without any conditions, be they financial, physical or mental commitments. Only your devotion is needed. Your devotion to your own practice every day according to your own time schedule, and arrangement and by your own free will. That is all that is needed.

Now, why is it that we could not keep the ancient disciplines left by the ancient Masters? It is not because we do not want to, or that we do not make any effort to do so. It is because we do not have enough power, we are tired, weary of existence. Sometimes we must work hard just to survive in this ever growing standard of civilization. And we also face even more 'civilized' temptations, so we must also adopt a more 'civilized' approach to guard ourselves if we want to regain our self-respect and wisdom. Because sometimes it looks like we are lost in the whirlpool of existence and pressure, and we seem to lose ourselves. Actually we do not lose our body or our desires, but we lose our self-control. This is why it is said in the Bible, '*What benefit is there for a man who gains the whole world and loses himself?*' [1]

But we do not really understand the meaning of losing our soul. We think, 'What? On the contrary, I lose nothing. I gain more and more every day.' If your employer gives you a promotion or if you decide to have another child, you only gain an additional small burden. Some burdens are bearable, others are adorable. And the more you engage in material activities, the more you lose yourself and the less you know yourself. And what should you know about yourself? Well, that we are the most powerful beings in the universe. All sacred scriptures talk about this. Buddhist texts state that human life is the most precious of all. Muslim scriptures say that we are guests on earth. This means then that our home is elsewhere, and that we are much more than our physical body.

But it isn't enough to believe it. You must follow a kind of personal training, and use your critical capacities and your wisdom to discover the superior levels of existence, and to adopt a more elevated way of thinking and living, that will transform you. Your internal power will do anything that you wish to accomplish. You will then know God and will be able to say, 'God acts through me,' and repeat what Jesus said, *I and my Father are one.* Then we will no longer feel loneliness and hardship." [5]

1 Matthew 16:26

6

Initiation

"*I*nitiation actually is just a word for opening the spirit. You see, we are crowded with many kinds of obstacles, invisible as well as visible, so the so-called initiation is the process of opening the gate of wisdom and letting it flow through this world, to bless the world, as well as the so-called Self. But the true Self is always in glory and wisdom, so there is no need of blessing for that." [53]

"Initiation means the beginning of a new life into a new order. It means that the Master has accepted you to become one of the beings in the circle of saints. Then, you are no longer an ordinary being, you are elevated, just like when you enroll for university, you are no longer a high school student. In the old times, they called it baptism or taking refuge in the Master." [36]

The Process of Initiation

"By the grace of the Master and by the God power inside, we get cleansed, even though we are not very pure at the time of initiation. We see light and hear sound when we break through the prison door, because they exist beyond the material existence. That is why we call it instant or immediate enlightenment. It means that at the time of initiation, we are in contact with higher worlds, and that we are no longer disconnected from them.

Let's say that it is a sunny day and you are in your house. If you do not open the door, you can't see the sun. Similarly, the light and the sound of God exist, but we are closed out in the prison of our own thoughts, prejudices and actions from many lives, and we cannot see or hear. During initiation, the Master gives us a chance to break through once and for all. But we have to keep going because there are many more levels to discover. Actually, initiation is only the beginning, although it is a great start because many people work from the lowest chakra up to the top one, and this can take maybe ten years, whereas we begin with the top one. The Master draws the whole power all the way to the top of the head so we can see the light. This (Master points to the Wisdom eye) is the door to Heaven, and you will go to many mansions.

When we transmit this method we do not even speak, and you will get the best enlightenment. You will get something you never had before, and you will feel something you never felt before, so light, so relaxed, so beautiful, so sinless. That is the meaning of baptism. When Jesus was baptized by John the Baptist, He saw the light that came down like a dove. So when we are baptized by a person that claims that he can baptize you, he must give you at least some light, just like this dove that came from heaven, or a light like a big flame that is mentioned in the

Bible, or you will hear the sound of God like the thunderous voice of God, or the sound of many waters. Then you are sure that you are baptized." [1]

"You'll hear the inner vibration or God's voice but without these ears, you'll see the light of God without these eyes. I cannot speak of it. You see, language and intellect belong to the realm of mind and matter (limited), not soul and God (unlimited). Our thinking arises from data, from learning, from other people's thinking. Our soul and God's nature are spontaneously self-born, self-existing, supporting and pure. So anything that is influenced by society, by thinking, by philosophy or by language belong to intellect and not to wisdom. So I can only transmit it in complete silence. This is why we call it mind to mind or heart to heart transmission." [22]

The Benefits of Initiation

"After initiation, the light from within will shine forth to show us the Kingdom of God, to lead us to our real Home. And we will find our true state of being, with such happiness that we never knew before in this world. We will overflow with all the beauty and virtue that we tried to cultivate, but never completely achieved before. The heavenly teachings through the inner language will revive all the wisdom that we possess, but were so far unable to use. Then, we will be the most satisfied person, and nothing in the world could offer the same effect." [52]

"After initiation, you have inside help and protection and also outside contact. Inside is when you meditate, you might see the Master helping, or you may see light, and feel good, comfortable and blissful. You will feel your wisdom growing more and more each day, and that your love expands to infinity. That is when you know that the method is successful, is very useful. Otherwise, how do you measure it, if everyone tells you to do something, to close your eyes and believe it, and offers you no proof? Proof, we must give you. Proof, you must demand. And you will have it at the time of initiation, immediately and continually afterwards, every day. You will experience miracles for yourself, when you are in trouble, when you have an accident, when you have no one to turn to. That is when you know God's power. That is when you know you love God. That is how you know that God is protecting and loving you. Otherwise, how do you know? How do we know that God exists? What is the use of God when we don't see Him, or don't see the protection and help when we are in need? We must feel that someone is there. So, that is how you worship God, even more as a Christian, after practicing the Quan Yin method, because we will know what God knows, we see, we feel, we experience the protection, the blessing power every moment of our life." [36]

Being a Disciple

"A disciple must remember God at all times, and God will be everywhere. We take some karma from people around us, by looking at them, by thinking about them, when sharing a book or a meal, etc. This is how we bless people and reduce their karma. This is why we practice, to spread the light and dispel the darkness. Blessed are those who give us some of their karma and we are happy to help them. We do not practice only for ourselves but for anyone crossing our path. This is why our progress is slow. Otherwise, we would go immediately to heaven, and who would bless the world after our departure? So we must stay here to pay our debt and bless the world. We are, after all, connected to each other. The people making roads, planes or our house, everyone receives some blessing from us. Just like the amount automatically deducted from your pay check for insurance, social security, etc. No way to escape! You can think of it another way. If you want to have a comfortable lifestyle, you will have to spend a lot of money to buy the new inventions and services society offers. So when we practice, people are automatically entitled to take a part of the result, of the merit. That is how five or six generations can be liberated, how your friends and your family members will be blessed when they die. These people are connected to you because they helped you, because you love them and they love you." [61]

"Most of our disciples, whenever they meet other disciples on the street or anywhere else, if they run into one another in a strange land, they just feel they are brothers, and they know they can trust that person. They know that person will help them, will love them, or at least will not harm them. Therefore, if the whole world is like this, what do you think? Of course, we still have our failures and our personalities, but we know we can trust each other, and we know we have love. We know we can give love. We know we give whatever we have. On this, we have confidence with each other. If we create a world like this, we don't need to go to heaven, we will stay right here. Therefore, we started with Nirvana and ended up on Earth. That is fine." [34]

"We have seen our true nature, the brightness inside, the greatness within, and when we talk to others, we have wisdom flowing out, and we feel that we know better now, and that we are truly near sainthood. But still, in some other moments, if we are not careful, we forget our greatness, we don't use our wisdom, and so it appears that we have fallen in the same habits of yesterday. Therefore, the precepts are there and the spiritual diary is there to remind us that we are the teachers of ourselves, anytime, always checking, always controlling, and always knowing when we stray.

You are as great as you make yourself to be. You are as great as you are, when you use your own greatness for the benefit of others as well as for self-enhancement. Otherwise, do not blame me if you don't see God, if you do not know your Buddha nature, if you don't know your Kingdom of God. It is you, yourself to be blamed. You are the one you should rely on to know your own greatness. I only point the way. It doesn't matter how great I am. You benefit nothing if you do not try to discover your own greatness and make use of it. Okay?" [43]

"Actually, we practice hard only to reach the point of relaxation, so that we can enjoy what we are and what we have in any circumstances, and so that we can open our hearts and tolerate anything, and feel the God-nature in all beings, so that we don't look down upon anyone." [62]

"After leaving this world, a practitioner of the Quan Yin Method will not have to be reborn again in this world, unless this person wants to come back as a Buddha to help relieve the suffering of mankind. It is because there are many more beautiful, extraordinary worlds for the practitioner of the Quan Yin Method to go. He has no need for this suffering world. His wisdom, his vibration, after practicing the Quan Yin Method has risen to a level of sainthood and it enables him to be fit to live in the glory of the Kingdom of God." [37]

"Do not always run around to take care of me. Take care of our guests, take care of our brothers and sisters or whoever needs to be taken care of. It is okay. Everyone likes to run around and take care of me, but you don't realize that I am in all of you. For you to take care of each other is like taking care of me. I only need a little amount of attention. I don't need all of you taking care of me, you will run over me! (laughter). You will overwhelm me with love and attention, and other brothers stand around and nobody takes care of them and it is me too, it is me who you left behind or didn't take care of. I feel the feelings of the person. You don't feel it, but I do. So if you don't take care of them, it means that you bother me, because I will know it, and I will be bothered." [60]

Q. Are you saying that the initiation is where you bless the person, and this opens them up for new possibilities?

M. Actually, we are the greatest in the universe, all of us. We came from the greatest source. Therefore, we must be the greatest. We can't just come from trees, rocks or anything we think of. So anyhow, the process of initiation is to immediately kind of shock us back into this highest position, which we have forgotten all along, because we have been too busy with daily mundane activities. [53]

Q. If one is initiated by you, do we remain your disciple forever? What is the job of a disciple?

M. The job of a disciple is to become a Master, so you don't need to be my disciple forever. You don't even need to be my disciple because you already are a Master, it's just that you do not know it. So I tell you how to recognize yourself again, that's all. [49]

Q. Would you consider initiating someone who has been initiated by another Master?

M. I would, but only if that person truly believes that I am more able to take her or him to a higher level and faster. Otherwise, it is better to stick to one's own Master, if one still feels much attached, and has much faith in that Master. If you believe that your Master is the best already, then don't change. If you still have doubt, and if you still have not gotten the light and sound which I have mentioned, then you should try. Because the light and the sound are the standard measurements for a real Master. Anyone who is not able to impart you immediate light or sound, is not a real Master, I am sorry to say. The road to heaven is equipped with light and sound. Just like when you dive in the sea, you have to be equipped with an oxygen mask and all that. There are things for different purposes. That is why you see saints with a halo of light around them. That is light. [38]

Q.   Why is initiation limited mostly to people under 65 years old?

M.   When we are a little older than sixty or sixty-five, our brain is no longer so alert. Yes? Most of the time, they cannot understand the Master's teachings. And the sudden change from flesh eating to a vegetarian diet might cause inconvenience at such an old age. You might not be able to follow the diet, is it clear? It is not that I discriminate against old age. If you are a long-time vegetarian already, or if your body is fit and you are willing to take a rigorous practice, every day for two and a half hours, morning and evenings, then of course I will also welcome you. But this is a general rule. [5]

Q.   How can children practice your method?

M.   When children are six years old, if they are with initiated parents, they can be half-initiated. When they are twelve, if they have parents who also practice, they can be initiated fully. If they don't have parents who are initiated, they have to wait until they are sixteen years old. [48]

The Five Precepts

"Our Wisdom-Eye at the moment is crowded with some obstructions made by our own ignorance and previous deeds of unvirtuous actions. To clean it we need the hand of someone who knows. We need a great power from God which we all have within us, if only we could open the 'tap' and then it would run out. It is like a water tank full of water, but with the tap obstructed. So if you wish, I can repair the tap for you, free of charge and free of conditions except that you should purify yourself, lead a virtuous life, and keep a virtuous diet. From today on you must vow to never take flesh again, never take any lives, never tell a lie, never steal, etc. It is exactly the same as the Ten Commandments of the Bible, or the five Buddhist lay precepts which say: Don't kill, don't tell lies, don't commit adultery, don't steal, don't drink alcohol, gamble or take drugs." [7]

1. Refrain from taking the life of sentient beings.

"Refraining oneself from killing also means not eating animal flesh because although we do not kill it ourselves, others have to kill so we can eat it. This is indirect killing. If we cannot keep the five commandments we cannot be born as human beings again.

Whenever we eat meat, it is unavoidable that some of the hatred, anger and frustration in the animal's heart caused when it departed, will be imprinted upon our consciousness, and then we will feel uneasy inside. Therefore, when we sleep at night we have nightmares, when animals see us they are frightened of us and run away. And when we are sick, it is difficult to heal ourselves because of all this hatred, this angry atmosphere which hangs around the meat that we eat." [5]

Q. Why can't we have products with animal fat? We can eat cheese, and there is fat in cheese?

M. Because cheese is made with milk, but fat comes from an animal that has been killed. And taking milk, we don't have to kill the cow, and from milk we can make cheese, butter, etc. This is the difference. [50]

Q. May we eat unfertilized eggs?

M. No, because the egg has half a life already, and if you give it a chance, it will become a chicken. Also, eggs will attract negative powers, ghosts, so if we eat some, we might get contaminated by these negative forces. As you may know, many black and white magicians use eggs to cure people who are possessed by spirits. So it is very logical not to eat eggs. [36]

Q. What if someone has the willingness to follow a vegetarian diet, but unconsciously or unknowingly eats meat? How would that affect him?

M. It would probably give you a little bit of a stomachache. But if you meditate a little bit more every day, and that would be no problem. We can't always avoid. The vegetarian diet is only to propagate more loving kindness which already exists in us. It is to polish it more, to bring it to its full extent, to all beings, including our younger brothers and sisters, to sow our love, and also to polish our compassion. But if we do something unconsciously, no one can blame us. God would not. [48]

2. Refrain from speaking what is not true.

3. Refrain from taking what is not yours.

"Whatever does not belong to us and we take it without permission or prior asking, that is stealing. We can steal people's time and energy also. You know this kind of stealing very well. Some friend phones you and talks for hours, and you just cannot stop it, and you get exhausted and out of politeness and compassion you just listen, 'Ah, yes, yes...' You don't know what they are talking about because they are so boring. This is also stealing. You should devote your time to knowing God instead of talking about useless topics."[5]

4. Refrain from sexual misconduct.

"Too much sexual abuse and indulgence tires your body, and exhausts your mental powers which should be conserved for the greatest enlightenment, and to help yourself and to help mankind. It is more noble that way. That's all. Sexual misconduct means you have too many girlfriends, too many boy friends, too many husbands and wives. It exhausts your storehouse of energy."[45]

"It is very simple, it means that if you have a husband already, please don't consider a second! Keep your life more simple, no complications and quarreling over emotions. It causes hurt feelings for other people. We don't harm other people, even emotionally. We try to avoid conflicts, try to avoid suffering emotionally, physically and mentally for everyone, especially our loved ones. That's all. If you already have a lover, don't tell him or her. It hurts more when you tell. Just solve it slowly and quietly, and don't confess to him. Sometimes, people think if they have an affair, and they go home and confess to their wife or their husband, that it is very wise and very honest. It's non-sense. It is no good. You already made the mistake, why bring your garbage home and let other people enjoy it? If he doesn't know about it, he doesn't feel that bad. The fact of knowing hurts. So we try to solve that problem and not to have it again, and that's it." [38]

Q. Do you respect homosexual relationships the same as you do heterosexual ones?

M. I don't know really, I am not expert in both.(laughter) All I can tell you is why do you identify yourself with the body and call yourself a homosexual or a heterosexual at all? We are not the body, brothers, we are the holy spirit. We are love incarnated, we are all wisdom, we are the Supreme Master of all things in the universe. Why do you identify yourself in such a manner, degrading yourself and making yourself feel inferior by classifying yourself as such and such. Know yourself as God, get enlightenment and all these things are just a matter of temporary transit.[41]

5. Refrain from the use of intoxicants.

"Intoxicants mean drugs, alcohol and all the things that make you become an addict, make a slave out of you, also blur your vision, damage your brain cells, and impair your ability to think, to see, and to do things clearly. These are intoxicants." [46]

"Smoking can slowly be changed, but should also be abstained from. We ought to be intoxicated by God's power and not by these cheap substitutes. Formerly, we were allowed to do that, or we might do that in ignorance, because we are unhappy and we are craving for something, but we don't know what it is.

We feel so empty inside, and we are unhappy despite all the money and civilized comforts. We feel somewhat unsatisfied, so we look for cigarettes, for drugs, for gambling, for sex, or whatever in order to satisfy ourselves. We think that we will satisfy ourselves, but the more we use them, the more we feel exhausted, empty and meaningless. The more you take, the more you crave for, and the more you feel abused in body and mind. The real "intoxication" will substitute for all of these, and make you satisfied, and you won't even want to do all these things."[7]

Q. If I am taking medications under a doctor's order, can I still be a vegetarian and be initiated?

M. Yes, sure, why not? Medication is not drugs. What I mean by drugs, you know, are the drugs that your country forbids. I also forbid them, for your sake, because it ruins your life, costs a lot of money, and makes you a dependent wretch. You should walk like a king, like a God on this earth, and bless the whole world with your greatest power and wisdom inside. [40]

Q. Why can't we drink alcohol since it is used in medicine?

M. Drinking affects our mind. It makes it cloudy and confused, and numbs our nerves to some extent. So, I do not care how good it affects you on the surface, because it harms your brain, and we have to rely on our thinking system to reach enlightenment. The more we numb it, the more confused we will become and we won't be able to think straight.[7]

Q. What about chemicals on fruits and vegetables?

M. Oh, my God! You are fanatic. Wash them with salty water, yes, and eat them. Otherwise, you will die, Hmm? [45]

Q. It is mentioned on the initiation sheet to never use spiritual power to cure another's illnesses. Could you comment on that? I live in a community where so many people do healing with their hands, and other types of healing.

M. You see, if you want to be a healer, then do healing. If you want to know the whole, including healing, then you must leave it for a while until you know the whole. Then you can heal. Heal without healing. People will just see you and get healed. You don't need to do any kind of mudra, or mess up their magnetic field. If you are successful in healing one person today, can you guarantee that he will not get sick tomorrow? You understand? It is not complete. And also, when a person gets healed by a spiritual healer, he believes in that spiritual healer, instead of believing in his own healing power within himself. That is dangerous for both, for the healer and the patient. The patient believes in the healer and the healer gets more ego. So the best way to heal a person is to become Christ. Heal without healing. Heal without knowing. [27]

Q. What do you mean by psychic healing being an obstacle to one's progress? If someone uses his hands to heal naturally with a method called Reiki, is this acceptable?

M. If you want to be fully enlightened, you must not interfere with other people's karma. Because by doing this, you will lose your spiritual force, and remain in the physical side.[51]

Q. Is it necessary to meditate two and half hours every day? Why?

M. We have to meditate two and a half hours because it is necessary to cleanse our soul, our infected areas, with a lot of elixir. Now, if you are dirty from a day's work, and you come home, you need two gallons of water, no less. Every day we mix in the world, and are infected by others, affected by everyone around us, and by our own unavoidable misdeeds. For example, when we breathe we kill a lot of invisible beings, when we eat vegetables, we kill vegetable lives. So the two and a half hours are like two gallons of water to wash our souls. If you wash with one and a half gallons, it is also okay, but you are not completely clean. Then tomorrow you will add again some more dirt, and you only clean with one gallon. Thus every day you are not completely clean, and you may smell one day.(laughter)[7]

Q. Regarding the five requirements you must follow in order to be initiated. What would happen if you do not follow them?

M. Then you don't. What else can I do? Try again, okay? If you think that it is good for you, and good for others, and it is like a protective fence around our spiritual sapling, then we keep them, and don't make damage to your just grown sapling. Otherwise, no one is there to condemn you, or do anything to you, except your own conscience. So try to keep to that, and whenever you fall, stand up and try again. [46]

Q. Why can't we mix other methods with the Quan Yin Method of meditation?

M. Concentrate and be one-pointed with my teachings in order to get the best result. If you meditate on my teaching and on money at the same time, or meditate on another mantra, of course you will be divided. This is very logical. I am not a dictator, I just tell you what is good for you. Whatever you want to do, you have to put all your attention on that point. People think that I am forbidding you this and that. No! Everything I tell you is just good advice, and the duty of a teacher. But of course you make your choice. If you do not follow me, it is okay. You are responsible for your actions, the success of your meditation practice, but I am responsible to tell you what is good for you. Okay? Everything I tell you is the age-old concentrated essence from practitioners who want to get away from the traps of materialism, and rise above this mind-matter controlling power, so that they can realize that there is something greater than their own body and their own machine or brain computer. So all these are like secret codes, or secret methods to speed yourself on the highway to spirituality. It is all your choice. The path of freedom is a path of responsibility, of self-responsibility. So I never impose anything, I just suggest. [54]

Vegetarianism

"We respect all lives in the creative Plan of God. We can see by ourselves that all lives resist suffering and resist death. Therefore, when we kill or see animals being killed, they are suffering and they try to run away. That means God empowered them with the instinct of wanting life. If we interfere and force their lives away, we interfere with God's will. We should treat every being in the same way as we ourselves like to be treated. Then our lives will be blessed with grace, with longevity and with wisdom. *'As you sow, so shall you reap.'* Then we will never blame God for any misfortune. The more we cultivate, the better we become in speech, in body and in mind." [20]

"Try to be as much as possible a vegetarian, it will help you. Even to be a vegetarian in a polluted area will help you be more immune, you must know that. Vegetarian people are less sick than the meat-eating people. It gives you protection, your mind will be calmer, and you will be thinking less. This is the good thing about a vegetarian diet. It is not only for its mercy quality. We forget that by not taking other lives, our life will also not be at stake. It is the law of karma, of cause and effect. If we forgive others, others will forgive us." [5]

"It is nice to have dinner without thinking that someone else had to suffer for it. This is the main reason for a vegetarian diet. You chose your own way of life, and chose less suffering for us, as well as for others."[60]

Q. Could you speak on vegetarian eating, and how this could contribute toward world peace?

M. You see, most the wars which happen in this world are due to economical reasons, prompted by the lack of food in different countries, and the lack of equal distribution of food. Now, if you care to read magazines and the results of research, then you will find out that to raise cattle and animals for meat consumption brings about an economical state of bankruptcy in all aspects. It causes the state of hunger in the third world. This isn't my conclusion. It is you, the American people, who researched and reached this conclusion.

Read about food processing and the book called DIET FOR A NEW AMERICA. The author is the son of an ice cream millionaire, and he gave it all up in order to be a vegetarian, and write a book against his family tradition and business. Such a stand means not only loss of money, but also prestige and business to him, but he did it for the sake of truth. But there are many more magazines and books giving you a lot of information and facts about vegetarianism and how it contributes to world peace.

You see, we bankrupt the resources of our planet to obtain flesh food, by feeding cattle so much protein, water and medicine. We use a lot of manpower, cars, roads, etc., and many hundreds of thousands of acres of land have been wasted before a cow can yield one meal. If all these resources could be distributed to the underdeveloped countries, then we could solve world hunger. When a country is in need of food, it will probably invade another country just to save its own people, but in the long run it creates bad causes and retributions. Remember what the Bible says, *'As you sow, so shall you reap.'* If we kill someone for food, then we will be killed because of food later. It is a pity that we are so intelligent, so civilized and yet most of us do not know the cause of the suffering of our neighboring countries. It is through our palate. In order to feed just one body, we kill so many beings and starve so many fellow human beings.

And this guilt, consciously or unconsciously will weigh down our conscience and make us suffer with incurable diseases such as cancer, tuberculosis, including AIDS. Ask yourself why the United States has the highest rate and suffers the most of cancer. Because we eat a lot of beef. We eat more meat that any other country. And ask yourself why the Chinese or other communist countries don't have such a high rate of cancer. They don't have meat. That is the conclusion of your research, not mine. So, do not blame me! [30]

Q. Must one become a strict vegetarian to become enlightened?

M. No, you don't have to. You can experience enlightenment without a vegetarian diet. But to be completely enlightened, and to keep the state of happiness all the time, we should grant happiness to all beings as well, in a complete way, give them no fear, have no threatening atmosphere around you. This is a more complete enlightenment. Being a vegetarian alone doesn't bring you enlightenment, or help you become a Buddha. All the cows and horses are all vegetarians, but that doesn't mean that they are enlightened. Vegetarianism is a great way for us to achieve complete enlightenment." [65]

Q. If I continue to eat meat, will I still have enlightenment after initiation?

M. Meat is the cause of all wars and suffering in this world, as well as in your personal self. To refrain from meat is to contribute peace to this planet. If we terminate the cause of killing, we will not reap the result of being killed or being wounded. Also, to refrain from eating meat is a non-direct action towards the *'Thou shalt not kill'* precept. Also, it nourishes our compassion towards all beings, so we can treat them as equal creations of God. Therefore, it is best that we refrain from animal products. Even if you are enlightened after initiation with a meat-eating diet, you will suffer a lot of heavy karmic burdens because it has to be cleansed out. And sometimes if you reach a certain height in spiritual attainment, you will experience some side-effects of your physical impurity when clashed with the absolute purity of Heaven. You understand? It is not always easy to withstand the intensity of power within yourselves, while having an impure physical and mental state of being. [49]

Q. Is fish okay to eat?

M. It is all right if you want to eat fish, but if you want to be vegetarian, fish is not a vegetable. (laughter) [30]

Q. In the Sermon on the Mount, Jesus fed thousands of people with fish and bread, and also at a wedding, Jesus turned water into wine...

M. So what is the question? You want me to know about this? I know. I have been asked a thousand times, and even if I didn't know, I would have to know by now! You mean that I say do not eat fish, and in the Bible it is said that Jesus fed fish to the crowd? But you must consider what kind of fish this was! He used two fish to feed five thousand people! It was a magic fish, made with air. [30]

Q. Do you feel that there is more aggression in societies that consume meat than in ones that consume less?

M. Yes. You can compare India with other countries that eat more meat. You can also compare the rate of aggression in religious communities that eat more meat than others, and then you will see the difference. You will also notice that animals that eat meat are more aggressive than herbivores. Even in the animal Kingdom, one can see the connection. [30]

7

Meditation

"Why should we meditate? To still our minds, in order to receive the teachings from heaven, from the Kingdom of God, or from higher worlds. We always keep praying and asking, 'Please give me wisdom, please give me that,' and then when God wants to speak, He has no chance anymore because we are busy all the time. We talk, we ask and we do not listen. Do you understand? So meditation is the listening time. Just like when you ask me a question, you have to be still for a while, quiet, then I have a chance to tell you what I want to tell, or what you need to know. Yes? So meditation is like this. Sit still and receive the message. Otherwise, God wants to tell you a millions things and you have no time to hear it. You are too busy talking, praying and singing, and prostrating, and counting the rosary. It is all right to do this. I do not mean that it is not good. It is very good, but then, we must be still for some time, so that God has a chance to communicate." [14]

"Peace has been within us all along. It is just that when we are too busy, seeking outside, we perhaps forget this real peace within us, and we encounter some uneasiness or difficulty in life. If we can somehow find the time, or the sincerity with which we can sit down, or just quiet ourselves down, and then search within ourselves, we will find this peace and happiness again. This is the true meaning of meditation. We don't really have to sit in a quiet corner of our house only. We can sit any-where, or stand in the bus station, or in the bus on the way to work, or sit where we work, and quietly search deep within our-selves for the true spirit which always exists. Because we are not the body or the mind. We are not what we are doing, or what we are learning, and we are not what we are brainwashed into believing that we are. This is difficult to explain. I just under-stand it clearly myself, and many of our fellow practitioners also understand it.

If we truly, even intellectually, realize or analyze even the one who we call 'I', or 'Mrs. Smith' or whatever we call ourselves, we will know clearly that we are not that. We have no existence, if that is the way we understand ourselves. If we think that we are the one with a lot of school knowledge, or the one who has anger when confronted with frustration or problems in life, or the one who is loving, who is satisfied with many successes etc., this is not the real 'we'. Before we were born we didn't have this knowledge of school degrees, or book-clinging wisdom, for example, and we didn't have this quality of anger, we didn't have this loving attitude, or the way we feel about pleasant things or reject unpleasant events, etc. So these are just habits, the knowl-edge that we accumulate while we grow up." [53]

"Everyone already knows how to meditate, but you meditate on the wrong things. Some people meditate on pretty girls, some on money, some on business. Every time you pay full attention, wholeheartedly, to one thing, that is meditation. Now, I pay only attention to the inner power, to the compassion, to the love, to the mercy quality of God. But it isn't by sitting cross-legged in a quiet place that one gets something. You have to be in contact with that inner power first and the real Self inside will meditate and awaken itself. That is our meditation. We must awaken the real Self inside and let him meditate, not our human brain and our mortal understanding. If not, you will sit down and think about a thousand things and won't be able to subdue your passions. But when you are self-awakened, the real inner Self, the God power within you, will control everything. You only know real meditation after you are awakened by transmission by a real Master. Otherwise, it is only a waste of time wrestling with your body and mind." [30]

The True Meaning of Meditation

"When you pray to your Father, enter your secret chamber and pray in secret and your Father will see you and reward you openly." [1]

"So, how do we pray in secret when we all go to church and pray openly? So maybe it isn't the way. The Bible teaches us not to pray loudly, like the heathen or the hypocrites do. So the secret lies in this secret chamber. That is why when we go to church, we pray a lot, out loud, and everyone hears it except God! So, most of the time, our wishes aren't fulfilled. It is because we do not follow what the Bible says. If we believe in it, then we should study it more carefully.

Now it isn't that we must sit there and think about God all the time. We just have to merge with God, and become one with God, and always be in His consciousness. That is what is meant

1 Matthew 6:5

by the Kingdom of God. If you go to the church once in a while, on Sunday, it is also a way to seek the Kingdom of God, but probably not a very fruitful way. Because Jesus said to us that the Kingdom of God comes not through observation, but it is within us. If it is so, what shall we do? Still, we must meditate, even though, it is said that the Kingdom of God doesn't come through observation, meaning not through meditation even. But it makes us more aware of it. The Kingdom of God isn't made by meditation, but by meditating we become aware of our Kingdom, which is already existing within ourselves." [30]

"Our meditation, we believe, is the original plan from God, that we should get in touch with the God power and with the Word of God. In the Bible it is said,

'In the beginning there was the Word, and the Word was God and the Word was with God.' [1]

So we meditate on that Word, which is the vibration within, the Word which indicates the frequency, the God Power. Because we are the temple of God, and God speaks to us in such a way. He appears to us in the form of light and speaks to us in the form of sounds. Seeing the light, we see many other things. Hearing the Word we hear many other things. We hear the teachings directly from God. So this is what we are meditating on. But when we have a powerful teacher, you may pray inside to Him or Her, if you have difficulty in meditation, or if you are too far from God, then you might need an intermediary. So you are still a little weak like a baby that needs his parents to hold him, so he can walk. But later you walk alone. You must know that your goal is walking alone, and growing up, and not to rely on parents forever." [22]

1 John 1:1

How to Meditate

"Simply turn your attention to where you should, to God, instead of money or other things. You already have the ability to meditate. Otherwise, you couldn't do your business, or take care of your children, if you didn't have any attention. So just turn it to the Kingdom of God. We will teach you more precisely with time. It isn't that the teaching takes a long time, it is only that the before and after procedures take time to explain. It is so you may know what awaits you on the way from here to heaven, on the different levels of consciousness. Therefore, it takes some time. Otherwise, you would just close your eyes and get immediately enlightened." [30]

"Beware of the openness of your energy while you meditate. But if we have a living teacher, whose energy is still alive, then he or she can protect you from this influence. But if we try to learn from a past Master whose magnetic field has drawn up to a higher dimension, we might have a little difficulty with asking for protection. We tend to pick up more easily the environmental influence, whether bad or good. So we can never be sure if that meditation experience is ours, or the neighbor's." [56]

Q.   Where can we meditate?

M.   Anywhere. In a park, in a garden, on a bus, on a plane, but not when you drive a car! You should not! (laughter) There are two kinds of meditations, one is on the inner light, and the other is on the heavenly music. In the latter case, you should meditate in private. It is better. I will explain every thing during initiation. [51]

Q.   How long should we meditate every day?

M.   It depends on how quickly you want to go to God. So, for ordinary people, maybe half an hour to an hour. But for our serious disciples, two and a half hours or three hours, at least. But then, after you become used to it, when you talk, you walk, when you sleep, it is just a kind of meditation all the time. And even when you sleep, you can see heavens and communicate with higher beings. [42]

Q. When meditating, how do we concentrate our thoughts without being affected by our daily life?

M. It will come naturally after some time of practicing. It will just be effortless. You won't even know when you think or don't think. You just sit there and it happens. The light will come, the sound will come, and you will be oblivious to everything. And whenever you want to come out of it, you will be aware of everything again. All right? It is very easy. [40]

M. What should we think about when we meditate?

Q. Nothing. We already think too much all the time, so why think again during meditation? But there is a way to calm our thoughts and our mind. I will teach you during initiation. We need time to sit down together and talk for a while During the real initiation, we won't be talking, including me, and in silence you will find your original nature. [49]

Q. Is it advisable for a person who has suffered mental problems such as severe depression and schizophrenia to practice meditation?

M. Yes. Yes, it is all right. It will cheer you up, and make you happy. You are depressed because you do not see God, you are separate from His love. Once you are connected with Him, and feel His presence and love, you will no more feel depressed. We are all depressed, some more, some less, because we are separated from God, and long to meet Him. Even if we have a lot of money, have a good wife or husband, somehow, we are never completely happy in this world. We always feel something is missing. Sometimes we also do things that are wrong, because we think that they will make us happy. It is only because we lack God's love. Therefore, when we are initiated and get in touch with God, we won't do wrong things again. It will be easier for us to keep the commandments, and love our enemies then, because we will have God's direct support. [9]

Q. You said that we are not to just go and meditate in a cave, but we are to be out in a kind of living, walking meditation in the world. Could you go into that in a little more detail?

M. After being initiated you will know how to meditate while living, and not to run away from the world. You will integrate this great cosmic power into your daily activities, as well as when you are meditating. You will accumulate it a little more consciously and dispatch it during your life, to benefit our world. Otherwise, there is no use to just meditate, and bless only yourself. Actually, when we know ourselves, we can bless the whole world. And after we are initiated and are enlightened, in whatever we do there will be a deeper meaning than just the surface physical work, and we will be having joy in doing our things, and not just doing our duty like before. And we will be able to contribute more and more, with less work. You see, I am a very small person, and I don't eat that much, and I don't sleep that much, but you say I am very active. It is because of this great energy. I would bust if I didn't do anything. (laughter) [53]

Q. You said that meditation will lessen desires and wants, but no matter how happy I am I still have many desires and wants. Can you explain why?

M. Maybe you don't meditate the way I meditate. I can't be responsible for that. When I say meditate, I mean the Quan Yin Method of meditation. We are in direct contact with our own source of all happiness, of all wish-fulfilling power, and then and there, you will be happier and with no wants. Ask all of my disciples. Of course, some of them get it slower because their level is different, but some get it quicker and eventually all desires just go. We don't reject things. 'Desirelessness' doesn't mean detesting everything in this life. It is not true, not true. We like things, we love things, we take care of things, but we are not attached to things. And should the things not be there as per our request, we are not bothered. Do you understand? This is the 'desirelessness' state. But this doesn't mean that you don't go out and make money. No, no, no!

Be successful, be as successful as you want to be. Work for it, use your wisdom inside to be more successful even. Earn as much money as you deserve and want, and if you can't use all of it, give it to me! (laughter) I can make use of it. I can give it to the victims of the volcanic eruption in the Philippines. I can give it to the Vietnamese refugees who have no clothes, no bedding, no mosquito nets, or to the poor in many other places.

No don't give it to me, I wouldn't accept your money. I am just joking! But should you not know what to do with it, I will tell you what to do. That's all. But you will use your money yourself. I don't accept any donations. [40]

Q.   How can we develop our Third Eye?

M.   You don't develop the Third Eye, because it is already there. We cannot develop what is not material. You see the Third Eye is just a way of speaking, because there isn't an eye at all. Normally we have two eyes, and we see things with a limited vision, but if we have the other eye, the Third Eye, then we can see things in the whole universe. That is why it is called the Third Eye. But actually, the soul doesn't need an eye to see, doesn't need ears to hear, or any sensory apparatus to perceive things. This is the highest Truth, the highest perception without having to use any fleshly instrument. That is our soul power, the Supreme Master within us, which knows all things, hears all things, in all ways, and everywhere. That is what we have to find, because we are that, the Supreme Master in all the universe. Can you imagine how great you are, and how you live your life now? That is why I feel very sorry for you, because you come here to listen to me, and you shouldn't have to do it. Because we are equal, we are exactly the same, we have the same power. It is a very sad thing. But you will know it, if you accept what I say, and you will know just what I know, what Christ knows, what Buddha knows. [41]

Q. When we sleep, our body is asleep, so who sees?

M. That is your soul, your real self. You are not your body. Your physical eyes cannot see anything without the power of the soul. Our body is, in a way, a prison, an instrument. We need a room to house the soul on this earth. Most often, after initiation, the Master arranges that we pay some of our karma through our dreams. That way, it is more comfortable. And sometimes you can also see the future. [24]

Q. Sometimes, when I meditate I feel very uplifted, but I don't see anything besides black and white. Does this mean that I am at a lower level, or that I am not that good yet?

M. If you see black and white, you should buy a color television! (laughter) You see, if you feel uplifted and more peaceful and more loving, more elevated and happy inside, that is the best result of meditation. All things pertain to bliss. You see, if we meditate and we see a lot of light and hear the sound, it is because we want to learn from the light and the sound, we want the wisdom of life, the peace and tranquillity of our soul. So if you have achieved peace and happiness, it means that somehow, you have already digested the blessing from the light and the sound. The important thing is that you have bliss, happiness and loving kindness, more and more every day. [43]

The Quan Yin Method of Meditation

"I thought I could share with you a little secret technique that I have learned and mastered, and maybe it could help you use your own greatest power, to help yourself, your friends, relatives, your nation and greatest of all, the whole universe. Because I have seen with my awakened eyes that all beings in the universe are linked together. We are all the same essence, we are only one. I have not read it from books only, I have seen this. Therefore, if you think that you are still in misery, that your life is not smooth enough, that God has forsaken you, that you haven't seen God with your own eyes, then please let us help you to find God." [15]

"Before I encountered this easy technique, I had tried many other techniques, like the Secret Doctrine of Tibetan Buddhism, or the Thai, or the Burmese etc. It was so complicated and boring for me. Maybe I am too small, maybe for you it isn't too tiring. But it was very time-consuming and you needed a lot of equipment and instruments in order to carry out this type of practice. But not with the Quan Yin Method. I found out that it was easier than anything else. You can sit in a train, in a bus, in a park, anywhere, and you can be in tune with God's power. You feel the protection and you can see God face to face. You may be in contact with Jesus, Buddha or with whomever you love most in your heart. They will appear to you, they may teach you something, they may protect you, guide you, hold your hand so your life will never again be lonely. But this is not even the highest state. The highest state, is that you become like Jesus, and then, you have all the power to save the world and to be safe from the misery and the round of birth and death. You become all-wise, all-knowing and omnipresent." [14]

"Our path isn't a religion. I do not convert anyone to Catholicism or Buddhism or any other 'ism,' I simply offer you a way to know yourself, to find out where you come from, to remember your mission here on earth, to discover the secret of the universe, to understand why there is so much misery and what awaits us after death. And every day you will see everything just like you see me now. I do not ask you to believe me, but to experience it every day for yourself." [67]

"The method is transmitted without words. If we use language to be enlightened, we are still in the intellectual realm and the mind will be wrestling and all this is very tiring. So I do not teach you a kind of mind-wrestling method because I think that we are tired enough from working every day, struggling with our problems, so there is no need to go home, sit cross-legged and wrestle again! You probably heard there were different methods leading to enlightenment, and indeed there are several. However, there is only one that can lead you to the highest enlightenment. You can take different paths at the beginning, but you will have to take this one to reach the top. This path must include contemplation of the inner light, and of the inner vibration that the Bible calls the Word.

"Know ye not that you are the temple of God and that the Spirit of God dwells in you?" [1]

1 Corinthians 3:16

So, we get in contact with this Spirit, which is a manifestation of divine light and vibration, and by doing so, we know God. In fact, it isn't really a method. It is the power of the Master. If you have it, then you can transmit it. The method is a transcendental one that cannot be described by our language. Even if someone describes it to you, you will not receive the light and the vibration, the inner peace and wisdom. Everything is transmitted in silence, and you will see your old Masters like Jesus or Buddha. You will receive all that you need to follow their footsteps, and little by little you will become Christ-like, and you will become one with God." [68]

"After I give you the Quan Yin Method, then you meditate, you try to search within yourselves to find what kind of power you have, what kind of capability you have forgotten, how much intelligence you have used, who you are, and what kind of position you have in the universe. You search and search, and you will find it." [34]

Q. Do the people who practice this method of meditation need to have a specific religious background or training? Do they have to belong to some particular form of religious belief?

M. No, not at all. They don't even have to have a religious background. They will be brought into the knowledge of Self, of greater spirit, and that is when they become truly religious. Religions are just some remnants, the leftover teachings from the ancient Masters, the oral teachings, the theoretical way of teachings, which every Master would have. One is the oral teaching, tell people this and that, and the other is to teach in silence, and this is the most important part. But the two parts combined together make a living teaching. Otherwise, it is only half. [53]

Q. What are the steps to enlightenment, and what level of enlightenment does this technique take you to?

M. It will take you to the source of all beings, where you came from, and where all beings will return. Between this earthly level and that absolute level, there are five levels of consciousness, or different planes of existence. And if we, through the practice of the heavenly light and sound and with the guidance of an experienced teacher, pass through these five levels, then we will arrive at the house of the Masters, where all Masters came from and return to after their mission, and where we also will come from in order to help other beings, should we desire to return to earth, or to any other earth planet in the universe. So the first step is to get initiation, and then, everything else will come. [47]

The "Word," the Inner Vibration

"Since immemorial times, music has been a must to mankind. Even animals feel attracted to music and plants are supposed to grow faster with it. Thus, if the outer melody is so important to all lives, the inner celestial, wondrous Sound is even more enchanting, and full of grace and blessing.

The fetus, while in the mother's womb eats nothing. Inside there is no air, no sunlight and he doesn't seem to mind at all. The reason being that he is in contact with the inner wondrous Sound, the source of all love, bliss and power. The fetus grows at an incredible pace under such conditions, and if it were to continue, he would be as tall as the sky after he is born. But after his birth, he is disconnected from this vibration, and he cries at the first contact with the outer world. No child has ever been born laughing. It is because he feels a great loss as the sound is severed from him.

There are two kinds of sound: the worldly sound, and the supra-worldly sound. The worldly sound is very important to our sensual and mental comfort, but the supra-worldly sound draws us back to God." [1]

"The Heavenly Music spoken of in all Holy scriptures of different religions such as the 'Word' in Christianity, the 'Shabd' in Hinduism, the 'heavenly music' in Chuang Tse, the 'Tao' in the Tao Te Ching, etc. are the only real teachings direct from the Kingdom of God. They are the language of universal love and great intelligence. All teachings come from the Silent Sound, all languages come from this universal language. That's why high level initiates on this path speak all languages within the soul sphere. That is the level of the Master, the one who has mastered the language of the Kingdom of God. We all possess this wisdom, the wisdom to understand all things above this shadowy world, to be omnipresent and to function as the most perfect being in the universe, if only we desire to remember again what we truly are." [52]

"This Word or divine vibration is mentioned in all religions. We call it Yin, others call it celestial music, Logos, Tao etc. It vibrates within all life and sustains the whole universe. This inner melody can heal all wounds, fulfill all desires and quench all worldly thirst. It is all-powerful and all-love. It is because we are made of this Sound that the contact with it brings peace and contentment to our heart. After listening to this Sound, our whole being changes, our entire outlook on life is greatly altered for the best. The wondrous vibration will cleanse off all undesirable traces of 'original sin' or what others call 'karma'. It is like a mighty river carrying along with its current all ugly garbage.

This Inner Sound is the great creative force of the cosmos. It sustains and nourishes all things. Its manifestation in the outer world can be heard in the natural melodies of the wind, the water, birds etc., which are the lower manifestations. There are however more subtle and higher sounds which are inaudible to our physical ears, because they vibrate at a higher rate than our material world. The way to these higher dimensions lies in the Sound itself, which we follow back to its original source. To hear higher sounds and see higher worlds, we must open and develop our higher senses. And to do this, we need a guide, a Master of the Way, who is like a travel guide who knows what lies ahead. Religious scriptures only describe these worlds, just like a land map. To really know the land, we have to get there in person. When we have a guide, then it is quicker and safer for us." [5]

"In the Buddhist scriptures it is mentioned that the Buddha speaks only with one language, but every being can perceive it according to his own understanding. Now this language is not the ordinary verbal language, it is a kind of sound, of inner vibration, that everyone can use to communicate with each other, and the Buddha can use it to communicate with sentient beings. If we think that it is the language of our world, then it is impossible. Because no matter how intelligent the Buddha is, He can only speak one language at a time. And it is impossible for all beings to listen to all languages at the same time, including animals and lower beings that also understand it. So this must mean the Word in the Bible. Also in Taoism, in the Tao Te Ching, Lao-tzu mentioned that this name we cannot name, the Tao cannot be explained, we can hear it without our ears, we can see it without our eyes, we can perceive it without our sense organs. Now this Word, sound or vibration, is the creative force of the universe. All the scriptures, if you read carefully, mention this Sound, and this so-called inner music." [6]

"So now, if we somehow can get in touch with this Word or sound stream, then we can know God's whereabouts, or we can be in contact with God. But what is the proof that we are in contact with this Word? After we are in contact with this inner vibration, our life changes for the better. We know many things we never knew before. We understand many things we never thought of before. We can do, accomplish many things we never dreamed of before. We are getting mightier, and mightier, until we become almighty. Our being becomes more capable and more enlarged until we are everywhere, until we become omnipresent, and then we know that we became one with God.

No one who comes into contact with this Sound or Word will not experience a great change in his or her life. This is what we call an enlightened person. The more we are in contact with this Sound, or the Quan Yin Method, the wiser we become, the more saint-like we become, and the less vexation, attachment, anger, hatred, and lust we will have. We will have more freedom, more love and peace, more wisdom, and everything we wish to have, including a more comfortable life. We won't only develop spiritually, but also materially, and in all aspects. We will feel much different than before.

With our poor worldly language, every time I would like to speak about this great treasure within us, I feel so ashamed of doing such a poor job. But I have somehow to try to convey a part of this great wisdom so that you may feel interested, and find it out for yourself, and then you will know it for yourself without any language." [1]

Q. Do you have dreams?

M. Yes, I have a dream. I dream that the whole world becomes peaceful, that everyone becomes a Buddha. I dream that all the killing will stop, that all the children will walk in peace

and harmony. I dream that all the nations will shake hands, protect each other, and help each other. I dream that our beautiful
planet will not be destroyed by some crazy atom bomb, a planet
that has taken billions, trillions of years to create in beauty and
love. Yes, that is my dream. [14]

A Biography of
Suma Ching Hai

Master Ching Hai was born in Au Lac (Vietnam). Her father was a highly reputed naturopath. He loved to study world literature and was especially interested in philosophy. Among his favorites were the writings of Lao-tzu and Chuang Tzu and these were available to Master Ching Hai as a young child. She read these and other philosophic texts from both the East and the West before she entered primary school.

Although her parents were Catholic, they were open to Buddhist thought. Her grandmother was a Buddhist. Master loved to spend time with her grandmother, and she taught her the scriptures and Buddhist worship. Master Ching Hai developed a very open attitude toward religion due to this background. She would attend a Catholic Church in the morning, a Buddhist temple in the afternoon, and in the evenings would listen to lectures on the holy teachings. This left her with many spiritual questions, such as "Where did we come from? What is life after death? Why are people so different?"

During the war, there was a shortage of doctors and nurses in her town, so Master helped in the hospital after classes. She washed patients, emptied bedpans and did errands in her efforts to ease people's suffering.

Master has always had a soft spot for animals, and would often take a wounded animal home, care for it and release it. When she saw an animal slaughtered, she would cry, wishing that she could prevent such unnecessary suffering. She has been a vegetarian, and has always been repulsed by the sight of killing or of meat, all her life.

She worked for a time in Germany as a translator for the Red Cross and also volunteered to work long hours in the service of Au Lac refugees. She did so at the expense of her own health and comfort. Her work with the Red Cross put Master Ching Hai in contact with refugees from many countries. She was continuously faced with the suffering and turmoil brought on by wars and natural disasters. Master suffered a great deal trying to alleviate the pain she saw, and she realized how impossible it was for any one person to stop the suffering of humanity. This drove her more strongly toward finding enlightenment, as she realized that only this could help alleviate mankind's pain. With this as her goal, she practiced meditation even more seriously. She sought out new teachers, read everything she could find, and tested many different methods. She felt, however, that these efforts were not working, and that she was not experiencing the spiritual phenomena she read about in the scriptures, nor was she reaching the enlightened state. This was extremely frustrating for her at the time.

While in Germany, Master Ching Hai was happily married to a German scientist, with doctorates in two fields. He was a kind, attentive and supportive husband. He became a vegetarian, traveled with his wife on pilgrimages and was very supportive of her charitable works. However, Master felt that she needed to leave her marriage in order to pursue her spiritual goals. She discussed this at great length with her husband, and their separation was with his agreement. This was an extremely difficult decision for both of them, but Master felt very strongly that this was the right decision. She needed to devote her undivided attention to the pursuit of enlightenment.

After leaving her marriage, Master sought to find the perfect method which could lead one to attain liberation in one lifetime. None of Master's teachers knew it, so she traveled and searched everywhere for the right Master. Finally, after many years, she found a Himalayan Master who initiated her into the Quan Yin Method, and gave her the Divine Transmission that she had sought for so many years. After a period of Quan Yin practice, she became fully enlightened. She continued practicing and improving her understanding, and remained in retreat in the Himalayas for some time.

Eventually, Master Ching Hai traveled to Formosa (Taiwan). One evening, during a typhoon with heavy rain, as she meditated in a room behind a small temple, a group of people knocked at her door. Master asked them why they had come, and they answered, "The Goddess of Mercy replied to our prayers and told us about you, saying that you are the great Master and we should pray to you for the method to reach liberation." Master tried to send them away but they would not go. Finally Master, touched by their sincerity and devotion, agreed to initiate them, but only after several months of purification and their agreement to adhere to a vegetarian diet.

Shy by nature, Master Ching Hai did not seek out students to teach. In fact, she ran away from people who sought her. This happened in India, in Germany, in Formosa and in the United States where she was living an unassuming life in a small temple. When she was "discovered" for the third time in Formosa, she realized that she must not run away from the inevitable tasks that lie ahead. She began sharing with all who wished to hear her message of Truth, and she began initiating sincere students into the Quan Yin Method.

Master Ching Hai's work has spread by word of mouth from this first small group in Formosa to many millions of people. She has traveled and taught throughout Asia, the United States, Latin America, Australia and Europe. Many people from all walks of life, and from many different religious backgrounds, have made great spiritual progress with her help. Grateful friends and disciples are to be found all over the world, ready and willing to help others learn from their beloved Master.

In addition to helping countless numbers of people through her spiritual teachings and initiations, Master Ching Hai has used her boundless energy to assist those who are suffering or in need. In recent years, her humanitarian efforts have touched the hearts and lives of millions of people all over the world. Master does not discriminate between suffering caused by spiritual ignorance, material privation, or circumstantial events. Wherever there is suffering, she will help.

Some of Master Ching Hai's humanitarian activities in the past few years include aid to: the homeless throughout the United States; victims of fire in southern California; victims of many floods in the Midwest United States, central and eastern Mainland China, Malaysia, Au Lac, Holland, Belgium and France; disadvantaged elderly in Brazil; those displaced by the eruption of Mt. Pinatubo in the Philippines; disaster victims in northern Thailand; destitute families in Formosa and

Singapore; lepers on Molokai, Hawaii; spiritual communities in India, Germany, and Uganda; families of mentally retarded children in Hawaii; victims of the Los Angeles earthquake; veterans of the United States; orphanages in Au Lac; institutions of medical research on AIDS and cancer in the United States; and many, many others as her work continues to this day. Of course, we must also mention Master Ching Hai's never-ending and tireless efforts to help the Au Lac refugees, those both inside and out of refugee camps.

Although she has not sought acknowledgment of any kind, Master Ching Hai has been recognized and honored for her humanitarian work by government officials throughout the world. For example, October 25, 1993 was proclaimed "Master Ching Hai Day" by the mayor of Honolulu Hawaii, and February 22, 1994 was likewise proclaimed by the governors of the States of Illinois, Iowa, Wisconsin, Kansas, Missouri and Minnesota. She also received the "World Peace Award" in Honolulu, and the "World Spiritual Leadership Award" at a ceremony in Chicago on February 22, 1994. Congratulatory messages were sent to the Chicago ceremony by many government officials worldwide, including Presidents Clinton, Bush, and Reagan. She was also bestowed the title "Honoured Citizen of America".

In recent years Master Ching Hai has also devoted herself to creative expression of the beauty she enjoys within. Her creative works include paintings, decorated fans, lamps, dress designs, and songs. Many of these items are made available for purposes of fundraising for chairity work.

Master Ching Hai has told us that she was not always enlightened. She lived a normal worldly life, and knows from experience about our problems, our heartaches, passions, desires and doubts. She also knows the Heavenly Realms of Buddhahood, and how to get there from here. Her sole function at this point in her life is to help us with our journey from the suffering and confusion of the un-awakened state to the Bliss and Absolute Clarity of Total Divine Realization. If you are ready, She is here to take you home!

Master Ching Hai takes an unusually broad view of all religions. She has studied and teaches the words of Jesus, Buddha, Lao-tzu and many others. She always emphasizes the similarities among the great teachings, and lets us see through her eyes how all the great Masters are preaching the same Truth. She often explains how different religious opinions have arisen, due only to the difference in opinions of different people in different countries at different times.

Master Ching Hai gives a variety of lectures to interested students, according to their backgrounds and cultures, including Christians, Moslems, Buddhists, Jews, Hindus or Taoists, etc. She speaks in English, French, German, Chinese, and Au Lac language. Those who wish to learn and practice the Quan Yin Method with Master Ching Hai are welcomed to receive her initiation.

Bibliography of Lectures

#	Date	Location
1	Mar 24-87	Peng Hu, Taiwan
	The Supra-Worldly Sound	
2	Sep 11-87	Lotung, Taiwan
	What Happens in Dying	
3	Feb 10-89	Malaysia
	The Six Buddhist Perfections	
4	May 24-89	San Francisco, CA, USA
	Why We Have to Find God Power	
5	May 25-89	San Francisco, CA, USA
	The Tao, The Sound, The Word	
6	May 27-89	San Jose, CA, U.S.A
	The Best Road to the Kingdom of God	
7	May 28-89	San Jose, CA, U.S.A
	Prepare Now for the End of Our Journey	
8	Jun 8-89	San Jose, Costa Rica
	To Disclose One's Inner Power	
9	Jun 9-89	San Jose, Costa Rica
	Jesus Was One of the Saviors	
10	Jun 15-89	Sao Paulo, Brazil
	Inner Sound Creates Boundless Love	
11	Jun 16-89	Sao Paulo, Brazil
	The Importance of Finding an Enlightened Master	
12	Jun 17-89	Sao Paulo, Brazil
	The Rescuer Exists Life After Life	

#	Date	Location
13	Oct 1-89	Malaysia
	Let Peace Begin with Us	
14	Oct 13-89	UC Berkeley, CA, USA
	Is God a Being or a Non-Being?	
15	Oct 15-89	Santa Cruz, CA, USA
	How to Find God	
16	Oct 20-89	U.C.L.A, CA, U.S.A
	Find a Proper Master	
17	Oct 21-89	U.C.L.A, CA, U.S.A
	Keep in Mind Who You Really Are	
18	Oct 27-89	Harvard, MA, USA
	The Eternal Life & the Universal Law	
19	Oct 28-89	Harvard, MA, USA
	The Difference Between Buddhism and Christianity	
20	Nov 29-89	Panama
	To Love God is to Keep His Commandments	
21	Feb 4-90	New York, NY, USA
	Good Attracts Good, Bad Attracts Bad	
22	Aug 13-90	Gilroy, CA, USA
	Interview with Michael Channin	
23	Feb 7-91	W. Virginia, USA
	Hare Krishna Conference	
24	Feb 24-91	Boston, MA, USA
	The Way to Gain the Kingdom of God is Through Enlightenment	
25	Mar 1-91	Los Angeles, CA, USA
	Broadcast USA	
26	Mar 6-91	United Nations, NY, USA
	What is the Cause of War and Peace?	
27	Mar 9-91	Boulder, CO, USA
	Moving Towards God Realization	
28	Mar 22-91	Seoul, Korea
	One Can Attain Enlightenment Anywhere	
29	Apr 10-91	Denver, CO,. USA
	Enlightenment is the Key Answer to Everything	
30	May 19-91	Stanton, CA, USA
	By All Means be Vegetarian	
31	May 29-91	San Jose, Costa Rica
	The One Who Realizes God and the Messiah of God	

#	Date	Location

32　Jun 2-91　　　San Jose, Costa Rica
The Truth About Buddha, Jesus Christ and the Real Enlightened Masters

33　Oct 18-91　　Tokyo, Japan
Everything is Created by the Human Imagination

34　Feb 23-92　　Penang, Malaysia
Start with Nirvana and End up on Earth

35　Feb 25-92　　Penang, Malaysia
Love and Care are the Duties of Human Beings

36　Mar 03-92　　Singapore
Create a Permanent Heaven for Ourselves and Later Generations

37　Mar 22-92　　Seoul, Korea
An Enlightened Person Does not Need to Forsake the World's Attainment

38　Jun 26-92　　United Nations, NY, USA
The Mystery of the World Beyond

39　Mar 9-93　　 Singapore
Back to the Golden Era

40　Mar 27-93　　Honolulu, HI, USA
Be Practical and Spiritual

41　Mar 28-93　　Honolulu, HI, USA
Be One with God's Wisdom

42　Mar 30-93　　Mexico City, Mexico
The Qualities of High Level Sentient Beings

43　Apr 6-93　　 Seattle, WA, USA
The Paradoxical Nature of Things

44　Apr 7-93　　 Seattle, WA, USA
Master's Power Brings Enlightenment

45　Apr 10-93　　Denver, CO, USA
To Appreciate Life Starts with Enlightenment

46　Apr 14-93　　Washington DC, USA
Enlightenment is the Tool for Everything

47　Apr 15-93　　Washington DC, USA
My Signature is in Your Heart

48　Apr 20-93　　U.N. Geneva, Switzerland
Let God Serve Through Us

49　Apr 24-93　　Paris, France
Rediscover Truth, Virtue and Beauty

50　Apr 25-93　　Paris, France
Sincerity is Essential for Meeting God

51　Apr 29-93　　Brussels, Belgium
God Gives the Most Beautiful Gift to the People of the World

#	Date	Location
52	May 4-93	Berlin, Germany
	Bring Heaven into Your Life	
53	10-19-93	Santa Cruz, CA, USA
	Interview Radio 2000	
54	11-12-93	Houston, TX, USA
	Masterhood Means Selfless Love	
55	11-25-93	Fremont, CA, USA
	Forgive Yourself	
56	11-27-93	San Francisco, CA, USA
	Have No Illusion About Enlightenment	
57	Nov-93	San Jose, CA, USA
	Interview with Do Van Tron (Radio Saigon)	
58	Aug 27-94	Austin, TX, USA
	Be Your Own Master	
59	Sep 8-94	Tokyo, Japan
	Save the World from Doomsday	
60	Nov 12-94	Houston, TX, USA
	Masterhood Means Selfless Love	
61, 62	Various Dates	
	Miscellaneous quotes from Suma Ching Hai monthly magazines.	
63-68	Various Dates	
	Quotes from unpublished talks, interviews, sample booklet etc.	

Index

How to Contact Us

The disciples of Master Ching Hai have established many Meditation Associations and Centers throughout the world. Liaison practitioners are located in major cities around the world. These practitioners have received initiation into the Quan Yin Method, and have volunteered to assist others who wish to either receive initiation or learn more about Master Ching Hai's teaching. They are ready to help you with your questions or to select the audio and video cassettes, and publications which would be most suitable for you.

To be added to our mailing list, to register for initiation or to receive a list of regional centers in the U.S., please contact us at the following addresses:

Africa

Suma Ching Hai
International Association
Johannesburg Center
5 Silas Str Cyrildene
Johhanesburg 2198
South Africa

Asia

Suma Ching Hai
International Association
Formosa Center
PO. Box 9, Hsihu
Miaoli Hsien
Formosa R.O.C.

Europe

Suma Ching Hai
International Association
Paris Center
11 Avenue des Champs Fleuris
93330 Neuilly sur Marne
France

Suma Ching Hai
International Association
Berlin Center
Kirschnerweg 2
12353 Berlin
Germany

Suma Ching Hai
International Association
Oxford Center
21A Riverside Road
Oxford, OX 2 OHT
United Kingdom

Suma Ching Hai
International Association
Valencia Center
Ave Perisy Valero 63-9A
46006 Valencia
Spain

Latin America

Suma Ching Hai
International Association
Costa Rica Center
P.O. Box 1044-1200
Povas, San Jose
Costa Rica

Oceania

Suma Ching Hai
International Association
Sydney Center
73 Jasmine Cres Cabramatta
NSW 2166, Sydney
Australia

United States and Canada

Suma Ching Hai
International Association
Los Angeles Center
PO. Box 10400
Westminster, CA 92685